THE ADULT ADHD

BLUEPRINT FOR DECLUTTERING, CLEANING AND ORGANIZING

AMY HARPER

Written by Amy Harper.
Published by Plural Creations LLC.

ISBNs:
EBook: 978-1-963174-21-2
Paperback: 978-1-963174-22-9
Hardcover: 978-1-963174-23-6

To my family, whose unwavering love guides me in all that I do—
thank you for being my steady light in life's stormy moments.

PREFACE

Hi,

I know firsthand how overwhelming it can feel to live in a space that constantly reflects the chaos inside your brain. For years, I believed something was wrong with me because I couldn't keep up—couldn't keep my house clean, couldn't keep routines in place, couldn't keep the shame from creeping in every time someone dropped by unannounced.

Then I realized the real problem: I was using systems that weren't made for brains like mine. That realization changed everything. I stopped trying to force myself into routines that didn't fit and started building systems that did. Slowly, my space became more manageable, and my nervous system could finally exhale.

This book isn't about having a perfect home. It's about building one that makes sense for you.

Whether this is your first step or your fiftieth, I'm honored to walk alongside you.

Amy Harper

TABLE OF CONTENTS

Interior design by Umer R. - behance.net/UmerRafaqat

INTRODUCTION

> You look a mess, Darling. You should really put more effort and care into your appearance.

These words from my mother cut like a sharp knife. As much as it was a blow to my heart, I understood where she was coming from. To the outside eye, it didn't look like I was trying... My hair was a mess, there were coffee stains on my not-so-ironed shirt, and I was 15 minutes late to the birthday brunch. But what no one saw, including my mother, was the internal battles I had fought all morning just to be there. My hair was a mess because I overslept after burning the midnight oil at work to ensure I made the deadline. The coffee stains happened as I ran out of the house, running late due to time blindness. And the being late? Well, on my way to the brunch, I drove past a flower shop and decided to stop and buy my mom her favorite flowers. Are these excuses? Not at all. It's simply my reality—the reality of living with ADHD.

Here's the truth:

Nobody wants to leave the house a mess.

I've never been early and thought, *No, this isn't on brand. Let's be late instead.* The state of my house, car, cupboard, and kitchen drawers isn't due to a lack of care or trying, and that's how I know that neither is yours. If you're an adult living with ADHD, I want you to take a deep breath and know this is a safe space for you to learn, be encouraged, and get equipped with organizing and cleaning tools that actually work for the ADHD mind. How do I know? Because, just like you, I've tried a thousand tools and techniques before that only worked for about five minutes. But through trial and error, loads of research, and using my professional skills, I've found ways to declutter, clean, and organize that work for my neurodivergent mind.

The tricky thing is that no two ADHDers are the same. What works for me might not work for you. So, what's the point of this book, right? While we're all different, there are certain building blocks that work for us all. I want you to imagine this book as all the ingredients you need to bake a cake. However, it's up to you to add some chocolate chips or strawberry filling to make the cake unique and exactly the flavor you want. The tools I'll share with you shouldn't be used exactly as they are. Instead, you should embrace the basic principles and feel free to customize them as much or as little as you see fit. Instead of rigid prescriptions, this book will provide you with frameworks, tools, and flexible systems to build what works for YOU.

THE PINTEREST DREAM

If you're like me, you have a Pinterest board (or three, because you forgot you already created two) filled with aesthetically pleasing homes where clutter doesn't exist. You know, those pristine homes where the kitchen can rival Martha Stewart's setup, the coffee table has nothing but a photo book and a funky-looking potted plant, and the bedroom looks like a hotel. I used to envision my life with a house like that, and I tried everything to achieve it. But allow me to share with you the hard truth: If you want a home that works for your ADHD mind, you should stop prioritizing aesthetics over functionality. The goal of this book is not to turn your house into a magazine cover. It's about making spaces work for your ADHD brain—starting right where you are. If you're looking for an aesthetically pleasing, miraculous cure, this isn't the book for you. But if you're looking for room-by-room systems, microhabits, and flexible plans that allow your brain to feel comfortable in your space, then this is exactly where you should be.

Why is it important to put the Pinterest dream on hold? Because we need to be realistic about our expectations if we want this to work. Instead of viewing organizing and cleaning from an aesthetic perspective, you need to adopt a more practical approach. This book is filled with evidence-informed and emotionally intelligent systems to help you function better and on your terms, not about perfection.

FROM CHAOS TO CONTROL

To help you paint a realistic picture of what to expect, allow me to take you on a little journey. Currently, we're at Point A. At Point A, you feel like your home is controlling you. There are piles everywhere, and nothing has a "place." You feel guilty, ashamed, and exhausted. You've probably tried cleaning systems before, but they didn't stick or made you feel even more overwhelmed than the clutter did. You dread having guests over, and you struggle to relax in your home. Trust me, I've been there. But now, I'm at Point B, which is where I want to take you.

At Point B, you're in charge again. You know where your things are and where they go. You have rituals, not routines. You don't feel panic when someone rings the doorbell, and you've built a system that works for you. Most importantly, you know how to get back on track when things start to go off track.

This book will guide you from Point A to Point B. Perhaps you're already somewhere in the middle, looking for additional help to get you across the finish line. Or maybe you've been stuck at Point A your entire life. Either way, allow this book to carry you toward a better place.

Here's what you can expect:

BEFORE	AFTER
I don't know where to start.	I have a plan and ritual to help me reset.
I feel embarrassed by my space.	I feel good when I walk into my space.
I can't keep my space clean.	I don't fear clutter anymore because I am in control.
I want a Pinterest-worthy home, and then I'll be happy.	I want a home that is practical and created to work for my mind.
I get overwhelmed when I think about my space.	I feel relaxed and comfortable in my space.

Table 1: Your present and future you.

SOUNDS GREAT, BUT HOW?

All of this might sound a little too good to be true. I get it. I've been there. So, let's make it practical by dissecting the "how." This book is structured in six parts. Each part is dedicated to a specific element of this journey, some more obviously necessary than others. We won't spend the same amount of time on each part, but all six parts are crucial to achieving the results you're looking for.

Here's a little breakdown of each section:

PART 1

UNDERSTANDING YOUR CLUTTER

Before we look at any solutions, we need to understand why ADHD and clutter often go hand in hand. Cluttering comes naturally to the ADHD mind, but it also makes it harder. In part one, we'll look at why that is and why it's not your fault.

PART 2

REWRITING THE RULES

In Part 2, we'll focus on replacing shame-based expectations with functional, neurodivergent-friendly strategies. Out with the aesthetics that look good, and in with the systems that will make you feel good.

PART 3

ROOM-BY-ROOM APPLICATION

In Part 3, we'll break down different areas of the house and tackle area-specific challenges with solutions that are ADHD-friendly. Instead of overwhelming you with a "one-size-fits-all" solution that won't have a lasting effect, we'll take the time to explore strategies tailored to each area.

PART 4

STICKING TO IT

The success of this journey lies in longevity. If a tool only works for a short period of time, we don't need it. The goal is not to provide a quick, one-time solution, but to bring about lasting change. That's why part four will focus on how to stick to the new ideas and solutions you've identified in the previous chapters. We'll focus on building a sustainable system without perfectionism.

PART 5
THE 7 DAY CHALLENGE

Part 5 will take all you've learned in the previous chapters and provide you with a seven-day challenge to reset your home. The goal is not to do a one-time clean and then have a perfect home forever. Instead, the seven-day challenge will focus on implementing tools on a daily basis, so it will provide lasting effects.

PART 6
RELAPSE- PROOFING

Since ADHD is cyclical, not linear, we need to be prepared for setbacks. Setbacks and relapses don't mean failure; it simply means we need to readjust and try again. In part six, we'll work together to create a plan of action for when relapse occurs so you won't be blindsided in the future.

With all the practicalities out of the way, I want you to know that I'm proud of you for taking this step and for being here. I know it's not easy. I know you've been misunderstood, mislabeled, and misrepresented all throughout your life, but I see you. I see you showing up. I see those coffee stains have good intentions behind them. I see your time blindness and distractibility. I see your intrusive thoughts, exhaustion, and shame. I see you. And this book is for you. It's not homework; it's a sandbox, filled with tools and toys to craft your life. So, get ready to build and sculpt the life you want and need. You've got this!

PART

01

UNDERSTANDING YOUR CLUTTER

"

The diagnosis of ADHD can be a gift. It explains why you are the way you are.

DR. EDWARD HALLOWELL

CHAPTER 1

ADHD AND CLUTTER—A NATURAL PAIR

> Having ADHD is like having a powerful race car for a brain, but with bicycle brakes. You need the right tools to slow it down.
>
> - DR. EDWARD HALLOWELL

Have you ever looked at the people in your life and admired how some things seem to come so naturally for them? My daughter is a natural at making friends and being empathetic toward every living creature. She knows exactly what to say to comfort her friends and brighten everyone's day. While some of her communication skills were learned over the years, she also has this natural way of talking that draws people in. Similarly, my best friend is a natural in the kitchen. I don't think she's used a single recipe in her entire life, as she cooks based on "feeling." I don't know how she does it, but every meal is master chef-worthy.

There was a time in my life when I was still in high school when it felt like cleaning and organizing came naturally to everyone but me. No matter how hard I tried, it seemed impossible to keep my school bag tidy and my closet organized. However, as I got older and learned more about the ADHD mind, I realized that organization didn't come naturally to everyone else—it was cluttering that came naturally to me!

It's one of the many ironies of ADHD: On the one hand, it's so easy to collect clutter. But on the other hand, our minds need a clutter-free space to thrive. It seems a little unfair, doesn't it? Well, we can either feel sorry for ourselves and hate the fact that clutter loves us, or we can equip ourselves with the right tools and mindset to manage it effectively. What do you say? Are you ready to take a closer look at why clutter and ADHD often go hand in hand and find ways to manage them? If not, it's too late. Let's do it anyway!

THE INVISIBLE BANNER

One of the hallmarks of ADHD is executive dysfunction. If you're brand new to the world of ADHD and have never heard these words, don't worry—I've got you. Executive dysfunction is a behavioral symptom that disrupts your ability to manage your actions, emotions, and thoughts (Cleveland Clinic, 2022). Long story short, it means that simple, everyday tasks are a little less simple and more challenging. When it comes to ADHD, executive dysfunction consists of three core aspects: impaired planning, limited working memory, and reduced impulse control. These three core aspects all contribute to your natural ability to clutter up a space. Let's explore each of these aspects a little closer to fully understand how they contribute to the clutter situation.

IMPAIRED PLANNING

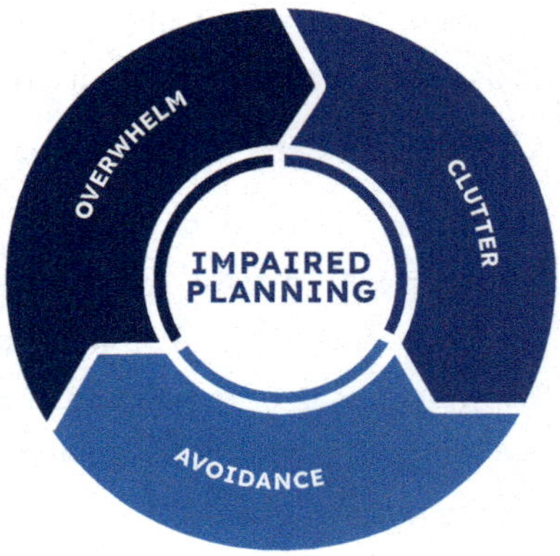

ADHDers often struggle with organizing tasks and setting priorities (no kidding), which leads to difficulties in initiating and completing simple household chores. Executive dysfunction can hinder your ability to analyze, plan, and organize tasks effectively (Russell, 2019). But what does that have to do with clutter? Have you ever had the intention to clean the living room but then felt overwhelmed by the magnitude of the task, so you just avoided that room for a couple of days? That's not because you're lazy or some other reason you might have blamed yourself for. It's because of your ADHD and executive dysfunction that goes with it. Because you experience impaired planning, it's much more difficult to set a task and complete it when you're feeling overwhelmed by its magnitude. Naturally, this overwhelming feeling and avoidance can cause clutter to accumulate over time, creating a cycle of clutter and avoidance.

LIMITED WORKING MEMORY

Working memory allows you to hold and manipulate information temporarily (Pugle, 2024). When it comes to ADHD, your working memory is a little limited, which is why you might start a task and completely forget that you started it. As a teenager, I often started cleaning my room. But then I would find a half-drank coffee mug and take it to the kitchen. On the way to the kitchen, I would hear the TV and decide to see what was on. And just like that, cleaning my room was a long-forgotten memory. Have you ever started cooking dinner but then got distracted by the dirty dishes and ended up cleaning the fridge instead? Before you know it, it's dinner time, and all you have to serve is a half-cut onion. According to research, lapses like these can easily contribute to clutter and disorganization, as tasks are left incomplete (Kofler et al., 2017).

REDUCED IMPULSE CONTROL

Impulse control issues can lead to acquiring items without considering their necessity, resulting in excessive possessions and clutter. Additionally, impulsivity can also cause you to start multiple tasks simultaneously without completing any. In some ways, your mind is like an adorable Golden Retriever puppy. One moment, you're completely content eating your snack, and the next, you're chasing across the lawn after the birds, only to get distracted again by the call you half-buried yesterday. It's important to view this aspect of your mind with kindness rather than judgment. You're not leaving tasks incomplete on purpose, and you're not acting impulsively because it's "quirky." It's how your ADHD mind works, and to ignore it won't do you any good (Stavraki, 2024).

These executive function challenges often result in scenarios where tasks are initiated but not completed, which ultimately leads to clutter. You might start the laundry but forget to transfer the clothes to the dryer, or begin cleaning a surface only to get sidetracked by organizing a drawer. Such patterns contribute to the "natural" cycle of clutter and disorganization. Now, I know this can evoke feelings of frustration, inadequacy, and self-criticism, as you might perceive yourself as lazy or incapable. But these negative feelings will only exacerbate the issue. Understanding that these challenges stem from neurological differences rather than personal failings is crucial for developing coping strategies and fostering self-compassion, which is exactly why we covered this topic before exploring practical strategies.

DECISION FATIGUE AND TIME BLINDNESS

Decision fatigue and time blindness are two common companions of ADHD. The best way to describe decision fatigue is by picturing the following. You're standing before a mountain of items: old magazines, mismatched socks, mysterious cables, and all the clothes you own. On paper, facing and organizing the mountain seems like a simple task, but each object demands a decision: *Should I keep this? Toss it? Where does it belong? What if I need this later?* These questions might seem straightforward, but they can accumulate rapidly and lead to a phenomenon known as decision fatigue (Cherry, 2022).

For ADHDers, decision fatigue is like having an app perpetually running in the background, draining mental battery life. The constant need to make choices depletes cognitive resources, making subsequent decisions increasingly challenging. This can culminate in task paralysis, where the brain, overwhelmed by choices, opts for the path of least resistance: doing nothing. It's akin to a computer freezing under too many open tabs. In other words, a simple choice can begin to feel like you're climbing Everest.

On the other hand, while having to climb Everest, you're also faced with time blindness. Imagine this: You glance at your phone and decide to scroll for five minutes. You scroll a little bit for what feels like five minutes, but when you catch yourself, it's been two hours. Just like that, two hours have *vanished*, and you're left wondering where the time went. Conversely, you might embark on a task, believing it will consume hours, only to find it wrapped up in fifteen minutes.

That is what we call time blindness, and it's the brain's faulty internal clock, making it challenging to gauge the passage of time accurately (Ovcharenko, 2025). It's like having a watch that speeds up or slows down unpredictably. As you probably well know, this can lead to chronic lateness, missed deadlines, or feeling perpetually behind schedule. So, what can we, as ADHDers, do about decision fatigue and time blindness? While we'll explore different kinds of organizational tools and skills later in this book, here's one way to streamline choices and combat paralysis.

DECISION TRIAGE

Decision triage is a strategy that simplifies or eliminates non-critical decisions, allowing you to conserve mental energy for more significant choices (Cherry, 2022). By creating predetermined rules or categories, you can reduce the cognitive load. For instance:

THE TWO-MINUTE RULE	If a task takes two minutes or less, do it immediately
PRE-SET CATEGORIES	When sorting items, have labeled bins: Keep, Donate, Trash. This reduces the need to deliberate over each item
SCHEDULED DECISION TIMES	Allocate specific times for decision-heavy tasks, ensuring you're mentally prepared and not already fatigued.

Table 2: Decision triage.

By implementing such strategies, you can navigate the maze of daily decisions more effectively, reducing the risk of paralysis and making tasks like decluttering more manageable.

THE SHAME SPIRAL AND AVOIDANCE LOOP

Have you ever felt like your clutter has developed a life of its own, multiplying faster than rabbits at a magic show? You and me both! This is the case for many ADHDers, where clutter isn't just about misplaced items but tied to a whirlwind of emotions. This whirlwind can lead to a self-perpetuating cycle known as the shame spiral and avoidance loop. Let's take a closer look.

THE BIRTH OF THE SHAME SPIRAL

It often starts innocently enough. A few dishes left unwashed, a pile of unopened mail, laundry that's more "floor-drobe" than wardrobe. But as these items accumulate, so does a nagging voice in your head: *I should know better, I'm too old to live like this*, or *What's wrong with me?* These internalized messages aren't just unkind; they can also become paralyzing. For ADHDers, this is merely about being messy. It's about executive function challenges that make organization daunting. The result? A profound sense of shame. As noted by Dr. William Dodson, "For many people with ADHD, shame arises from the repeated failure to meet expectations from parents, teachers, friends, bosses, and the world" (ADDitude Editors, n.d.).

ENTER THE AVOIDANCE LOOP

Shame is a heavy burden, and the natural response is often to avoid its source. This avoidance can be overt, such as deciding that the cluttered room is now off-limits, or subtle, like draping a blanket over a chaotic desk or immersing oneself in endless hours of screen time to distract from the surrounding disarray. But here's the kicker: avoidance doesn't solve the problem. In fact, it often makes it worse. The clutter remains, possibly grows, and so does the shame. It's a vicious cycle where clutter leads to shame, shame leads to avoidance, and avoidance leads back to more clutter (Courage Compass Therapy, n.d.).

However, it's crucial to recognize that this cycle isn't a reflection of laziness or a character flaw. Shame is often intertwined with deeper issues like years of untreated symptoms or childhood trauma. Avoidance is your brain's way of saying, *This feels too big to deal with right now.* To break the loop, start with compassion. Name the cycle (*Oh hey, it's the shame spiral again!*), share your struggle with someone safe, and start small. One drawer. One box. One moment of clarity. Small steps can lead to big breakthroughs.

ADHD VS. NEUROTYPICAL APPROACHES

Most organizing advice sounds something like this:

1. Start in one room.
2. Sort items into categories of deep, donate, or toss.
3. Put everything in labeled bins.
4. Repeat until your entire house is picture-perfect.

Sounds reasonable, right? Except if you have ADHD, this advice might feel like trying to build IKEA furniture blindfolded, with missing screws, and also you're on fire. Here's the thing: Most traditional organizing systems are built for neurotypical brains that thrive on linear steps, abstract categorizations, and delayed gratification. ADHD brains, on the other hand, often process information in a more associative, emotionally reactive, and nonlinear way.

So while someone else might be able to think, *This goes in the office closet*, and walk there calmy, you might pick up the object, remember the office is a mess, open the closet, get overwhelmed by the stack of boxes, notice an old yearbook, sit down to flip through it, and three hours later you're traveling through high school memories while surrounded by a bigger mess than you started with. But that's not a lack of willpower, it's the reality of executive dysfunction.

That's exactly why this book approaches things a little differently and will incorporate visual cues over linear logic. The ADHD brain loves visual information. If something is "out of sight," it's often "out of existence." Closed drawers = forgotten stuff. Labeled bins behind cabinet doors? As effective as hiding things in another dimension. This is something I've experienced many times. I've tried organizing my pantry with a million matching containers, only to promptly forget where I put the quinoa and continued to buy three more bags. So, instead of having matching containers with pretty colors, I switched to clear containers with bright labels on an open shelf, right before my eyes. And you know what happened? Not only did I find the quinoa, but I used it—on purpose.

That's why this book will focus on ADHD-friendly systems, which means they are:

FLEXIBLE	Because every day isn't the same
VISUAL	Because you need to see it to remember it
IMMEDIATE	Because we want short-term wins and not long-term theories
LOW-EFFORT TO MAINTAIN	Because burnout is real.
PERMISSION-BASED	Because systems don't have to be the best, they just need to be good enough

Table 3: *ADHD-friendly systems.*

So, let's leave this chapter with a big, bold truth:

Clutter is not moral failure.

CHAPTER TAKEAWAYS

01 Executive function is like an invisible banner. You want to get organized, but your brain keeps throwing up stop signs. It's not laziness; it's that your mental wiring makes planning, prioritizing, and follow-through feel like wading through molasses in roller skates.

---

02 Decision fatigue and time blindness are clutter's BFFs. Even "simple" choices can add up quickly and send you into a mental shutdown. Add in time blindness and suddenly, it's tomorrow and the pile's still there.

---

03 Clutter often comes with a side of shame. The mess isn't just physical—it carries emotional weight. Thoughts like "I should know better" or "I'm too old to live like this" sneak in and make it harder to begin. But that shame? It's a learned response, not a personality trait.

---

04 Your clutter is not a moral failure. ADHDers aren't lazy, messy, or incapable of "adulting." The problem isn't your motivation—it's that traditional organization advice doesn't work for how your brain is wired.

---

05 ADHD-friendly systems must match how *you* think, move, and function at your best. What works for neurotypicals isn't going to cut it. You need strategies tailored to your energy levels, attention patterns, and how your brain processes the world.

CHAPTER 2

THE EMOTIONAL TOLL OF LETTING GO

> ADHD is not a deficit of attention, but rather a challenge of attention regulation. The ADHD brain pays attention to everything; the challenge is paying attention to the right things at the right time
>
> - DR. THOMAS E. BROWN

A lot of people think decluttering is just about stuff. You know, junk drawers filled to the brim with receipts, mismatched socks, and that one mysterious box in the garage labeled as "important." So, it may come as a surprise to many that the most challenging part of decluttering for ADHDers isn't sorting or cleaning—it's feeling. If you're anything like me, ADHD brain and all, you know exactly what I mean.

I've held onto a sweater I never wear because my grandmother gave it to me. I've kept college notebooks because I thought, *What if I need to prove that I once knew how to do calculus?* Spoiler alert: I'm still waiting for that day. I've saved countless trinkets from people I don't even talk to just because tossing them felt... wrong.

For many of us with ADHD, clutter isn't just clutter. It's memories. It's guilt. It's little pieces of identity scattered around the house like breadcrumbs from who we used to be or who we think we should be. But here's where it gets really sticky:

Letting go can often feel like we're letting down someone or some version of ourselves. I remember when we moved houses many years ago. I had such a hard time letting go of the most random things just because someone else had given them to me. It's almost as if I believed they would somehow sense in their being that I got rid of it and would be hurt by my actions.

There are many reasons why certain items are harder to let go of than others. To avoid dealing with those reasons, we tend to shut the drawer and promise to deal with it later. Only later never comes. In this chapter, we're going to talk about the stuff that makes you cry in the back of your closet. The items that whisper, "You're a bad daughter if you get rid of this," or "You'll never be that productive again." But we're also going to learn how to face them with compassion, not shame.

Because here's the hard truth:

Holding on doesn't make you loyal, and letting go doesn't make you cold. The goal of decluttering isn't to erase your past but to stop letting it pile on your floor.

Let's embrace this chapter gently. No pressure, no judgment. Just you, me, and a little emotional honesty with a side of two trash bags.

EMOTIONALLY CHARGED CLUTTER

It's time to talk about some heavy stuff. And no, I don't mean the heavy boxes in the attic... We'll get to those later. I mean the kind of clutter that hits you in the chest. The items that seem innocent until you pick them up and suddenly feel a lump in your throat or a wave of regret. You freeze, and the decluttering session you were pumped for screeches to a halt. If you've ever found yourself staring at a box for 30 minutes because it contains feelings, you've run into some emotionally charged clutter.

For ADHDers, this stuff can be particularly sticky. We feel things deeply and often all at once (Barkley, 2010). Combine that with time blindness, working memory issues, and a love-hate relationship with the past and the future, and it's no surprise we form strong emotional attachments to objects (Brown, 2021). In my own decluttering journey and in helping so many other ADHDers, I've noticed four primary "flavors" of emotional clutter that sneak up on us. Maybe you'll recognize them, too.

GRIEF ITEMS

After my dad passed, I couldn't throw away his coffee mug. Not because it was a great mug—it was chipped and the handle was weird—but because *he* held it. It sat on his desk during Sunday crossword puzzles and late-night chats. It was the mug he sipped from slowly when I asked him if I was allowed to go to the dance, the mug he held in his hand when he told me that he had a surprise for me in the driveway (my very own car). To me, that mug was more than just a mug: it was grief in ceramic form.

Grief items are the items that make you feel like letting go is losing them again. They are items tied to something we've lost, whether a loved one or a different version of ourselves. It could be a wedding dress after a divorce, baby clothes from a child who's grown up, or keepsakes from a friendship that faded. For ADHDers, emotional memory is often stronger than chronological memory, making these items powerful emotional triggers (Hallowell & Ratey, 2021). We keep them because we fear letting go of the thing means letting go of the person.

IDENTITY ITEMS

Raise your hand if you've got a stack of sketchbooks even though you haven't drawn in years. Or running shoes that saw more Instagram than pavement. Yeah, me too. These are identity items. Things that represent who we used to be or who we aspire to become. For people with ADHD, our interests can burn hot and fast (hello, hyperfocus) and then fade away, leaving a trail of half-finished hobbies behind (Kaufman, 2021). The result? Closets full of costumes from former lives. Letting go of identity clutter can feel like admitting failure. But here's a reframe: those items aren't proof you failed. They're proof you were curious, hopeful, and human. And you're allowed to evolve.

GUILT ITEMS

One year for my birthday, my aunt gave me a wooden box with green felt on the inside to keep fancy cutlery pretty. I loved the gesture, but I hated the box. I don't even own fancy cutlery, so I was in no need of a box for it. I also knew I would forget about whatever was inside the box the moment I tried to use it. So, the box stayed in my closet for many, many years because, well... guilt.

Guilt clutter shows up as gifts you never liked, expensive items you regret buying, or things you feel you should use but don't. It's that voice in your head saying, *I spent money on this*, or *They'll be hurt if they find out I tossed it.* Here's the truth: Gifts are acts of generosity, not obligations to hold onto something forever. If something makes you feel guilty every time you look at it? It's not a gift anymore. It's emotional debt.

ASPIRATIONAL ITEMS

These are my personal kryptonite. I once had six different types of yarn, two sewing machines, and a closet full of "goal weight" clothes... and I don't knit, sew, or like the color of half those outfits. Why did I have all those things? Aspirational clutter.

Aspirational clutter is the stuff we keep for our future selves. The books we plan to read, the hobbies we might take up, the clothes we'll wear once we "get our act together." For ADHD brains, this category stings the most because it's wrapped in hope and self-judgment. It's also a tough one, because time can feel fuzzy. We're constantly living in the shame of not yet: not yet skinny, not yet productive, not yet worthy of the life we imagined (Matlen, 2017). But let me tell you something: Your worth isn't hiding inside a dusty knitting kit. You don't have to earn your space by becoming someone else. Recognizing emotional clutter is the first step to letting go *without* feeling like a monster.

TECHNIQUES FOR COMPASSIONATE DECLUTTERING

You've faced the emotional clutter dragons—grief, identity, guilt, and aspirations—and lived to tell the tale. First of all, high five. That's not easy. Now, let's shift from *why* this is hard to *how* we can make it easier. If you're like me (ADHD brain and tender-hearted hoarder of "maybe one day" sweaters), you desperately need decluttering tools that do more than sort socks. You need systems that get how emotionally messy this can be. You need a system that offers structure without pressure, choices without overwhelm, and progress without perfection.

Below are a few of my favorite go-to strategies. They're designed to give your emotions space while gently guiding your decisions. And yes, they totally count as "doing the work," even if you only get through one drawer:

THE 30-DAY BOX

For: guilt, grief, and identity items

Sometimes, we just need *time*.
That's where the 30-day box comes in.

Here's how it works:

1. Take the items you're unsure about and place them in a clearly labeled box.
2. Write today's date plus 30 days on the lid.
3. Put the box somewhere out of sight—but *not* buried in Narnia.
4. Put an alarm on your phone to check the box after 30 days, but don't open the lid.
5. If you don't open it within the 30 days, ask yourself: *Do I even remember what's in here?* If not, you may be ready to let go.

This technique helps bypass decision paralysis by giving your brain a gentle pause, rather than a hard yes or no. It's especially useful for people with ADHD, because it externalizes the decision-making process—removing the item from your environment quiets the emotional noise long enough to gain clarity (Barkley, 2010).

THE KEEP/HONOR/ARCHIVE/LET GO METHOD

For: identity, grief, and aspirational items

This is my all-time favorite sorting method because it lets you keep meaning while making space. Use bins, laundry baskets, or even color-coded sticky notes.

Here's the breakdown:

- **Keep:** items you love, use, or need right now
- **Honor:** symbolic items you'll display or store intentionally (think: a frame-worthy photo or one beloved letter)

- **Archive:** items that are important but don't need to be in daily rotation (these go in labeled bins or memory boxes)
- **Let go:** items that no longer serve a purpose or spark joy (yes, Marie Kondo was *onto* something)

This method turns decluttering into a creative act—curating your life, rather than just purging it. It also works well with ADHD brains, because categorizing by *emotional role* is often easier than by function (Brown, 2021).

THE MEMORY CAPSULE

For: grief, identity, and guilt items

Think of this as a time capsule, but for *you.* It's a single shoebox (or a small bin) where you place the most special, most meaningful items that you *just can't part with.* The rule? Once the box is full, you have to edit to add more.

This creates an emotional boundary. It allows you to keep treasured items while also practicing limits. For ADHDers, who often struggle with object permanence and emotional regulation, this tiny structure can feel oddly freeing (Hallowell & Ratey, 2021). You get to say yes to your memories—just not to *all* of them.

> **Tip:**
>
> Decorate the box if that helps. Make it a mini shrine, not a clutter graveyard.

If you're still holding onto something that hurts, that's okay. The goal isn't perfection; it's progress with kindness. Every item you sort, every drawer you finish, every "maybe later" box you create? It's one step closer to making space not just in your home, but in your head.

CHAPTER TAKEAWAYS

01 Emotionally charged clutter is real and valid. ADHD brains often associate feelings with objects, making decluttering an emotionally intense experience. You're not being dramatic; you're being human.

02 Not all clutter is just "stuff." Items can represent grief, identity, guilt, or aspiration. Understanding why something is hard to let go of is the first step toward doing it with compassion, not shame.

03 You don't have to decide everything right now. Tools like the 30-Day Box and Memory Capsule create space for reflection, helping ADHDers manage overwhelm while still making progress.

04 Decluttering isn't about perfection—it's about peace. By using gentle, structured methods like Keep/Honor/Archive/Let Go, you can clear space without bulldozing your emotions or your history.

05 You're not failing—your system just needs a rewrite. The emotional toll of clutter isn't a sign you're broken. It's a signal that your environment needs to better reflect how your brain processes memory, emotion, and meaning.

PART

02

REWRITING THE RULES

"

ADHD is not a disorder of not knowing what to do, but a disorder of not doing what you know.

RUSSELL BARKLEY

CHAPTER 3

DITCH PERFECTION

> With ADHD, you have a kaleidoscope mind, always shifting and changing.
>
> - ANONYMOUS

Okay, friend. It's time to take a deep breath because we're about to say goodbye to an old, very pushy houseguest who's been overstaying their welcome: perfection. If you're anything like me, then you've probably spent a lot of time imagining the perfect version of your space. You know, the one from Pinterest and those dreamy YouTube makeover videos with floating shelves and minimalist jars with not a single stray sock or ADHD pile in sight... But here's the truth: That vision is often more paralyzing than inspiring.

Perfection is like a judge friend who whispers things like, "Why even bother unless you can't do it right." And then your brain, already juggling executive function like a circus act, goes, "You're right. I guess I'll just do... nothing." That's why this chapter is all about ditching perfection. It's not because you don't deserve a beautiful space, but because when you're managing ADHD, the goal has to be realistic and not idealistic.

In this chapter, we'll reframe what "done" looks like, what "clean" means, and who you're actually doing this for (Spoiler: It's for yourself and not your neighbor Karen). We'll introduce a new concept: the idea of something being "clean enough." We'll also look at why clarity beats aesthetics every single time.

But before we get into it, I want you to know that this isn't about lowering the bar. It's about building a bar that fits your brain. When we let go of perfection, we make room for peace, and trust me, that's a great trade. Let's do this, messy hair and all!

CLEAN ENOUGH

Let's play a quick game called "Is it dirty or just... visible?"

Here's the thing: A lot of us ADHDers grew up absorbing ideas about "clean" that were less about function and more about performance. Like, if someone popped by unexpectedly and there were crumbs on the counter, you'd instantly spiral into *I am a disaster human and must not be trusted with houseplants or responsibilities.* But can I be real with you?

> You don't live in a magazine shoot. You live in a space that holds your life, which includes breakfast crumbs, your creative projects, your kids' socks that multiply like rabbits, and the list goes on and on.

A couple of years ago, a family friend of ours shared a hilarious story: As an intern at a marketing agency, he was excited to be invited to take part in the food photography shoot they had scheduled for a client. In typical intern fashion, he was tasked with running around and grabbing different equipment from various rooms as the shoot continued. The photos looked amazing, and once everything was finished, his manager casually mentioned that everyone was allowed to take some of the food for themselves if they wanted to. The family friend waited until everyone else had taken what they wanted, and to his surprise, the waffle with cream and chocolate was still on the table.

He didn't ask questions; he was all too grateful that the waffle was still available and took a big bite. At first, the texture seemed different, and then the taste kicked in... "What's in this?" he exclaimed as the office roared with laughter. "Oh, we forgot to tell you. We use shaving cream for the photos. It looks better than real whipped cream," one of his colleagues shared.

Just like the family friend felt bamboozled by the food photography using inedible ingredients to make it look better, many house and lifestyle photos we see online are, well, *fake*. We see the perfect, clean home, but little do we know it's actually a set or a hotel, not someone with a real life living there. Or perhaps we're comparing ourselves to people who have seven maids on the daily! It's unrealistic, and that's why we need to find what is "clean enough" for us. So, what is it? Clean enough is whatever supports your brain and your life, not someone else's Instagram reel.

DEFINING YOUR CLEAN ENOUGH

Our definitions of 'clean enough' can also differ from one another. In fact, it should be. It needs to be personal to *you*. This is what my definition of clean enough looks like: If I can walk barefoot without stepping on anything painful, find my keys in under 60 seconds, and have a comfy spot to sit with my coffee, my house is clean enough. If it smells fine and there's a clear-ish path to the door? Victory. Is it perfect? Nope. But does it work for my ADHD brain? Absolutely!

To find your version of clean enough, let's reframe the conversation with some gentler, more useful questions. In each space of your home, ask yourself:

What do I actually need to do in this room? (e.g., eat, relax, dance like no one's watching)

What kinds of mess stress me out the most? (Visual clutter? Dirty dishes? Paper piles?)

What mess is actually harmless, or even helpful? (Like a bin of toys left out because it keeps your kid occupied)

Now, think about your thinking. What clutters your mind more than your space? Are you stressed about mess because it bothers you, or because you're scared someone will judge you? The goal shouldn't be to please the Clean House Police. It's to reduce stress and make daily living easier for you.

REAL LIFE EXAMPLES

Let me paint you a few totally functional, ADHD-friendly scenes. While these scenes might have been painted as "forbidden" in the past, I want you to realize that they are normal and okay. Remember, we don't live in a magazine!

- First up, I want you to imagine the good old half-covered dining table. There's mail on one side, crayons on the other, and in the middle, it's clear enough for Taco Tuesday. It's still a dining table, and it's still functional. You need the mail to be visible to remember to pay the bills. And you want your children to feel allowed to live in their own home, hence the crayons.

- Next, let's look at the visible bin system where every living room has open baskets labeled "chargers," "remotes," and "random stuff I'll deal with later." Is it pretty? Not really. While it might look cluttered to some, you know where everything is, which is an ADHD success.
- Lastly, picture the clean corner strategy. It's where you pick one area of the house that always stays clear, even if the rest is in chaos. It might be your favorite chair, your bed, or a desk in your home office. That one clean space is your reset button, and while the rest might be in chaos, you can find peace in your clean corner.

These three examples aren't cop-outs. They are strategies. ADHD-friendly spaces often look different because they function differently, and that's totally okay (Matlen, 2017).

Ditching perfection doesn't mean giving up. It means letting go of standards that were never designed for your brain in the first place. Clean enough is not a consolation prize. It's a victory that looks different on every ADHD battlefield. Celebrate your version of clean and reclaim your space. Remember, a little mess isn't a sign of failure; it's a sign that life is happening, and that's beautiful.

CLARITY OVER AESTHETIC

I love traveling! One of my favorite trips ever was when I traveled to France with my daughter. While I was there, I bought a set of adorable, matching storage boxes with French script labels, like "souvenirs" and "miscellany." They were cream-colored, stackable, and very Instagramable. You know what I put in them? I have no idea. Because within a week, my ADHD brain forgot what was inside, and since they weren't see-through and the labels weren't functional, I just kept adding more stuff. They became somewhat of a Bermuda Triangle.

Anything I didn't want to deal with or think about, I added to those boxes. As you can imagine, that system failed spectacularly. The thing is, when it comes to ADHD, we need to value function over aesthetics. In our world, clarity is king.

Neurotypical organization tips often lean on minimalism, uniformity, and aesthetics—basically, "hide everything, label nothing, and make it look like no one actually lives here." But for ADHDers, if we can't see it, we forget it exists (Matlen, 2017). We need our stuff to be visually accessible, or it might as well be in a different realm. So, let's stop designing our spaces to impress imaginary guests and start designing them to support our brains. To help with that, allow me to introduce you to strategies that saved my sanity—and at least four pairs of missing scissors.

- **Open baskets:** Forget lids. Lids are the enemy. Open baskets let you toss stuff in quickly and still *see* what's there. I've got one in the entryway for keys, sunglasses, and that one reusable bag I always forget.
- **Clear bins:** Whether it's pantry items or craft supplies, if I can't see it, it doesn't exist. Transparent bins are magical. You know what's inside, and it actually invites use instead of mystery and abandonment.
- **Visual zones:** Designate parts of a room for certain activities. In my living room, the couch corner is "Rest Zone," and the table near the window is "Creative Mess Zone." It keeps the chaos somewhat contained and makes cleanup more intuitive.
- **Color coding:** Give different types of items their own color. For example: red folders = bills, blue = work, green = personal stuff. Your brain will start associating categories with colors, which is way easier to track than reading tiny tabs when your executive function is on lunch break (Brown, 2021).
- **Simple labels:** Labels don't need to be cute or cryptic. They need to tell your brain what's what *fast*. "Charging Cable" is better than "Tech Hub." Trust me. When you're feeling overwhelmed, putting an empty coffee mug in the "tech hub" box might make sense because surely they drink coffee there, right? Keep it short and clear.

The moment I stopped chasing pretty and started choosing tools that matched how my brain operates, my space became more peaceful, and ironically, more stylish. There's something kind of beautiful about shelves that show off your stuff clearly and bins that make sense at a glance. Let's stop pretending Pinterest knows your life better than you do. Design isn't about performance; it's about support. And support should feel like a deep breath, not a deep clean.

Why don't you take a minute right now and ask yourself the following questions:

What parts of my current space look nice but don't actually work for me?

Where do I lose track of things the most?

What's one swap I could make to improve my life? (For example, swapping your old organized bins with clear bins)

When your system makes sense at a glance, you use less energy managing your stuff and more energy living your life. That's not cutting corners—that's designing for how your brain works. And that, my friend, is functional beauty.

REMOVING THE PRESSURE TO IMPRESS

Have you ever had that nightmare where someone shows up at your house uninvited? Or they let you know they'll be there in 15 minutes? There's a special kind of panic that kicks in when this happens. You know, the one where you're sweating through your shirt, trying to make it look like no one lives in your house, just in case someone judges your unfolded towels or your "temporary" clutter pile that's been there since last spring.

Here's a crazy thought: Your home is for you first. Not your mom. Not your judgy neighbor. Not your well-meaning friend who decorates seasonally and alphabetizes her spices. Just you. Here's a little secret from years of working with ADHD clients and from being one myself. The stuff we obsess over? Most people don't even see it. You're panicking about the crumbs on the counter while your guest is just grateful you offered snacks. You're spiraling because your towels aren't rolled like in the hotels, while your guest is trying to remember if they locked their car. We can get so stuck in believing our spaces have to be performance-ready when really, people come over to connect, not judge (Matlen, 2017). And if they *are* judging your home? That's not your problem. That's their problem.

It took me a while, but here's what finally clicked: When I started organizing for my comfort instead of someone else's approval, everything changed. My systems got simpler. I stopped hiding things in pretty containers that would later confuse me. I created drop zones and open shelves that worked with my energy patterns, rather than against them. And through all these changes, I began to feel calmer, more focused, and even a little proud. Not because it was perfect, but because it worked. To help you set priorities for energy and ease, ask yourself these few questions:

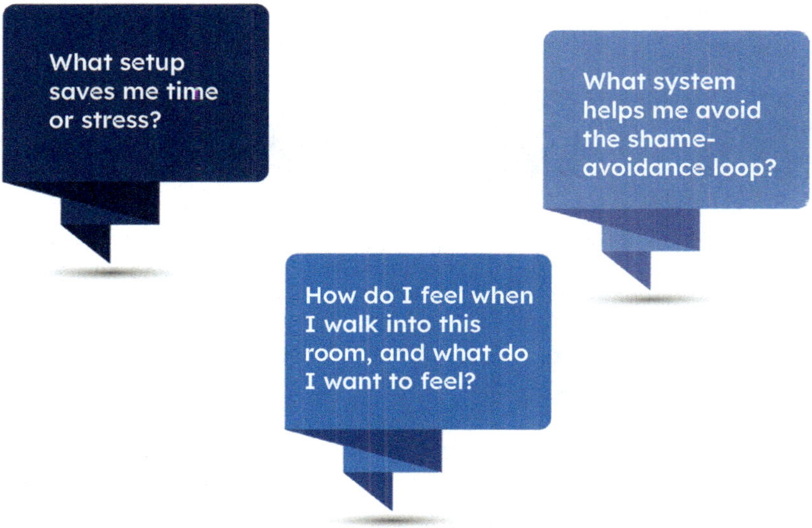

Allow these questions to guide you, instead of the classic *Would this impress my old high school rival if they dropped by unexpectedly?*

POSITIVE MANTRAS

To help remind you of the change, I suggest placing some positive mantras around your home where you can see them daily and be reminded of your goal. When you feel like the need for perfection is taking over, repeat one of these mantras over and over again, until you feel centered and at peace once more. Here are a few examples of mantras to help reframe the goal.

- Comfort over compliments.
- Calm over curated.
- My space, my pace.
- Function before form.
- Done is better than perfect.

To make it visual, here's a table for swapping aesthetics with ADHD-compatible wins.

AESTHETIC GOAL	ADHD-COMPATIBLE WIN
Matching labeled bins	I can see and reach what I need easily
Clear counters all the time	Designated drop zones to prevent chaos
Hidden storage everywhere	Open baskets or shelves for visual recall
Tidy entryway shoes	Shoe tray that catches the mess on purpose
Uniform closet hangers	Clothes I actually wear are visible and ready
Cute label fonts	Big bold labels I can read across the room
"No mess" rule	10-minute daily resets that keep it manageable

Table 4: Aesthetic vs ADHD-compatible wins .

Releasing the pressure to impress doesn't mean giving up. It means owning your space and your needs. A home that supports your brain, your energy, and your actual daily life? That's not just ADHD-friendly. It's liberating! Forget the aesthetic fantasy and embrace functionality. It's so much more sustainable and satisfying.

CHAPTER TAKEAWAY

01 Clean enough is a personal standard and not a universal rule. Your home only needs to work for you.

---

02 Function always trumps form for ADHD brains. Clear bins, bold labels, and visual zones are not lazy; they're strategic. Design your space to match your brain, not someone else's mood board.

---

03 Your home is not a showroom. Release the pressure to impress. Guests notice hospitality more than your clutter.

---

04 Organize for energy and emotional ease. Systems that save stress are more valuable than ones that look perfect. Choose setups that support how you move, think, and live daily, not just how they appear in a snapshot.

---

05 Reframe your goal and choose calm over curated. The real win isn't a perfectly folded towel. It's about being able to find what you need, breathing easier, and feeling good in your space.

CHAPTER 4

THE THREE-PHASE SYSTEM

> Sometimes, I feel like my mind is a television set that has too many channels on at once.
>
> ANONYMOUS

If chapters had subtitles, this chapter would've been called "How to Stop Cleaning Like a Tornado and Start Working With Your Brain Instead." Tell me if this sounds familiar: You get the sudden urge to clean everything. Fueled by either panic, caffeine, or a wildly optimistic YouTube video, you dive in. Fifteen minutes later, you're surrounded by open drawers, half-sorted piles, a stack of "I don't know" items, and zero idea where to go next. Your motivation fizzles, and you end up rage-scrolling in a room that's somehow messier than when you started.

Yeah. I've lived that moment more times than I can count. That's why I stopped trying to "clean the whole house" and started working in phases—clear, doable, ADHD-proof phases that work with how our brains operate. The truth is, we ADHDers don't struggle because we're bad at cleaning or organizing. We struggle because we're trying to do it all at once, in a system designed for someone else's brain. But when we break things down into manageable steps that build on each other, we get something magical: progress that sticks.

In this chapter, I'm going to introduce you to what I call the three-phase system. It's a flexible, ADHD brain-friendly approach that will help reset visual chaos before it overwhelms you, clean in layers that feel doable (and perhaps even fun), and organize in a way that feels intuitive, not like a puzzle that you have to resolve every time you need a pen. Because life with ADHD rarely goes exactly as planned, there's also a bonus section on how to adapt the system based on your energy, mood, or available bandwidth. Let's be real: Some days, you're a productivity unicorn, while other days, it's a miracle you remembered to eat.

So, are you ready to ditch the all-or-nothing cycle and find a flow that actually fits you? Let's get into it!

PHASE 1: DECLUTTERING WITH VISUAL RESETS

Let's talk about one of the hardest parts of decluttering: starting.

For ADHD brains, "Where do I begin" is not a simple question. It's more like a panic spiral in disguise. *Should I do the kitchen junk drawer? The laundry mountain? That one mystery bin in the hallway that might be full of wires, receipts, or old snacks?* When everything feels equally urgent and equally overwhelming, we freeze. Cue the executive function traffic jam. That's where a visual reset comes in.

This phase isn't about tackling your entire home. It's about reclaiming what you can see, because visible clutter isn't just stuff. It's visual noise. It nags at your brain every time you pass by, draining energy and fueling that low-key shame hum in the background. So, what do we do? We start with the obvious wins. Think kitchen counters, dining tables, entryways, or your chair of doom. The goal isn't to clean everything, but rather to provide some relief by reducing the visual chaos that keeps you from even wanting to begin. To help you with this phase, here are four of my go-to tools for a visual reset.

THE 15-MINUTE SURFACE SWEEP

Set a timer for 15 minutes. Pick one surface to tackle. And GO!

You're not solving the whole room—you're just cleaning that one countertop or that table. Grab a laundry basket or box to toss anything that doesn't belong there (we'll deal with the box later. Future you is capable). When the timer goes off, stop. You win!

THE RULE OF THREE

Feeling stuck? Choose three visible areas to reset. That's it. Clear them one at a time: your desk, the floor around your bed, and the hallway. More than three and your brain might start to short-circuit. But three? That's totally doable. Once you're done, celebrate the win, and tomorrow (or whenever you're ready), choose the next three.

THE RELOCATE BASKET

Keep one laundry basket nearby to serve as a catch-all for out-of-place stuff. This keeps you from running around the house mid-clean, chasing distractions. One basket equals one task. You'll rehome items later, or when we get to Phase 3. For now, simply pretend you're a farmer, walking through your field and picking up anything that is out of place.

STICKY NOTE ZONES

Use sticky notes to label temporary zones. For example, a note that says "To sort later," or "Keep here." This wil give your brain permission to move on without overthinking each item. ADHD brains love external cues because it's like borrowing executive function from paper (Davis, 2022).

So, what makes Phase 1 successful? Let's reframe what a win means during this phase. If you cleared the three counters, that's amazing. If you made one surface feel calm, you're on track. If you got distracted but managed to relocate a few things? Still a win! Remember, the process is layered. Phase 1 isn't about the final product. It's about resetting your environment just enough so you can breathe easier and move forward without getting bogged down in decision loops. You don't have to declutter your whole life in a weekend. You just need to clear enough space to make thinking easier. That's the magic of a visual reset.

PHASE 2: CLEANING IN DOPAMINE-FRIENDLY LAYERS

Here's a not-so-secret secret:

Most of us with ADHD don't hate cleaning. We hate how it starts boring, stays boring, and ends with us on the floor googling whether it's safe to vacuum a paper clip.

The trick isn't to power through like a cleaning robot. It's about building momentum in layers and letting each layer be enough if that's all you have in the tank today. I call this layered cleaning (very creative, I know). Think of it like making a lasagna. You don't need the sauce, cheese, and herbs just to enjoy the noodles. Sometimes, a basic noodle layer is dinner. It's all about the layers, so let's dig into them one by one.

LAYER 1: TRASH AND RELOCATE

When you're ready for a Phase 2 cleaning, always start with this step. No spray bottles. No scrub brushes. Just grab a trach bag and a laundry basket. Toss what's obvious trash, like empty cups, receipts, wrappers, and broken pens, and relocate what doesn't belong. Take that laundry basket filled with things from Phase 1 and begin to put them where they belong. If you don't get through the whole basket, that's okay. A start is better than nothing.

Layer one is surprisingly powerful. Just removing the noise of out-of-place items often reveals that the room isn't as dirty as it felt. For a lot of us, this step alone reduces overwhelm enough to keep going (Matlen, 2018). To make this layer even more appropriable, add a few small details to boost your dopamine levels. How on earth can cleaning be made fun? Well, here are three ways that I boost my dopamine during this phase:

- Blast a throwback playlist that makes you want to dance between trash pickups.
- Use a trash bag in your favorite color (yes, I have pink trash bags).
- Light a candle before you start and trick your brain into thinking something special is happening.

LAYER 2: WIPE AND SWEEP

This is your functional clean layer. It doesn't require a lot of detail. The goal is simply to make things feel usable again. After you've removed the trash and relocated the belongings into the laundry basket, it's time to grab some basic cleaning supplies and remove the dust and dirt. During this layer, you should wipe counters and tables with whatever cloth you've got handy. Sweep up the visible crumbs and dust bunnies (don't worry about the hidden corners), and give the bathroom a quick wipe. If you're short on time or motivation to do anything productive, do the basics only, like wiping the toilet seat and the edges of the sink.

This layer gives maximum impact for minimal effort. It's also where the ADHD brain tends to find rhythm. You've already moved around in Layer 1, so your engine is idling, and now you're simply cruising. But if that's not the case, don't worry. Here are a few things you can do to boost your dopamine levels during this layer:

- Use a cleaner that smells good and makes you want to spray it. I love lavender vinegar or anything citrus.
- Try a novelty cleaning tool, like a handheld mini-vacuum or a fun-colored duster. Remember, the ADHD brain loves novelty (Barkley, 2011).
- Pretend you're on a game show called "Can I Wipe This in 60 Seconds." This helps me tremendously! I've competed in many "challenges" over the years, and it's my go-to when I'm feeling unmotivated.

LAYER 3: DETAIL CLEANING

The final layer is like the sprinkles on top of the ice cream. If you're feeling focused or riding the dopamine wave, go ahead and vacuum the corners, polish that mirror, or wipe down the baseboards. But if you want to stop after Layer 2, you can. You've still done the job. This layer is for you, not for the invisible judge who might pop in for inspection or peer through your blinds. If you want to do a thorough, detailed clean, here are a few ways to keep your dopamine levels flowing:

- Set a five-minute timer and challenge yourself to detail-clean one thing.
- Reward yourself afterward with a snack, screen time, or a standing ovation.

One of my clients, Laura, used to think cleaning meant "top to bottom, one and done." She'd avoid it for weeks because it felt like a five-hour ordeal. Once we switched to layered cleaning, she started doing ten-minute resets a few times a week, and now her house is cleaner than it ever was under the all-or-nothing method. Her words, not mine: "I didn't change how I cleaned. I changed what I counted as a successful clean." Preach, Laura!

Cleaning in layers works because it gives you multiple stopping points, built-in permission to pause. That's not laziness. That's scaffolding your attention in a way that honors your brain's rhythms (Davis, 2022). Each layer is progress. Each layer counts. And hey, your home doesn't need to sparkle to feel good. It just needs to feel livable to you.

PHASE 3: ORGANIZING FOR FRICTIONLESS USE

During this phase, we'll focus on making life easier for "future you." After you've cleaned the surfaces, wiped, swept, and even spritzed a little citrus cleaner while dancing in your socks, the room is no longer yelling at you. Nice! But now comes the final—and dare I say, most freeing—phase: organizing. Not for Instagram or imaginary house guests, but for you. Specifically, the version of you who will be rushing out the door in mismatched socks tomorrow morning. We're building what I like to call "frictionless systems." These are systems that are so easy, so intuitive, they practically run themselves. No overthinking. No re-stacking. No pulling out seven bins to get to the one thing you use.

Remember, the ADHD brain loves what it can see, what's easy to grab, and what doesn't require a multi-step ritual just to access the tape dispenser. So, that's what we organize around. One of my favorite mantras I use daily and teach my clients is: "Organize around behavior, not ideals." If your keys always end up on the kitchen counter, no matter how cute the tray by the door is, then guess what? The kitchen counter is the new key zone. It's not a failure of discipline but an invitation to build smarter systems. Don't fight it, but embrace it.

How can we build frictionless systems and embrace the tendencies of our mind? Start by putting stuff where you use it. Keep the mugs next to the coffee machine, the pet stuff near the back door, and the chargers in the spots where your devices usually run out of battery life.

> The closer the distance between storage and action, the more likely you are to keep using the system (Davis, 2022).

When it comes to the ADHD mind, what you see is what you'll use. If we can't see it, it might as well not exist. That's why, when organizing, it's vital to use clear containers, open baskets, and labeled zones instead of opaque bins, sealed boxes, and guessing games. Now, this doesn't mean you have to label every drawer like a kindergarten cubby. But a few sticky notes or icon labels can anchor your brain to what lives where. A good rule of thumb is this: If something takes more than two steps to retrieve, it's probably not going to last long-term. Build your system with future-you's attention span in mind.

I once spent an entire Saturday alphabetizing my spices into tiny matching jars with custom labels. It was beautiful. It was Insta-worthy. It was also the last time I touched the spices for about four months. Why? Because when I cook, it's chaos, and I usually don't have time to read small labels or guess whether it's cinnamon or ground cumin. So, what did I change? I divided my spice rack into two open containers. One labeled "cooking stuff" and the other one "baking stuff." I also reverted back to the original packaging since I knew a green lid meant it was some sort of grassy herb. Now, I can actually cook, without rage or bland food.

Something similar worked for a client of mine, Josh. He loves going to the gym and kept trying to store his gym gear in the hall closet. Yet, it always ended up on the couch. The solution? Move the gym bin beside the couch rather than keeping it in the closet. Now, there's no more guilt and no more tripping. Just acceptance and ease. To create a frictionless system, you need to keep these three core things in mind:

- Honor your natural behavior.
- Keep it visually obvious.
- Don't create a system that requires daily maintenance.

BONUS: ADAPTING BASED ON ENERGY AND MOOD

I want to tell you a secret: I don't always finish what I start. Gasp! I know, scandalous for someone writing a book about cleaning and organizing. But here's the thing—ADHD isn't about a lack of effort, but about a mismatch between energy, interest, and timing. That's why I teach every single client this golden rule:

> You don't have to do everything, you just have to do what fits your energy right now.

So, here are a few bonus tools to help you find the right cleaning mode depending on where you're at.

WHERE TO START

It's vital to start where you are, not where you think you should be. Too many of us try to jump into deep-cleaning mode when our brains are running on low battery. That's a one-way ticket to burnout and Netflix avoidance. Instead, I suggest choosing your entry point based on your current mental and physical state. Here's how:

LOW ENERGY	You're in "visual reset mode." Just tidy the surfaces you see. Or literally toss trash into a bin while listening to your comfort podcast. Or don't move at all. Light a candle, breathe in that citrus-peppermint blend, and mentally prepare to maybe pick up a sock. This counts.
MEDIUM ENERGY	Try a 10-minute burst. Pick one drawer, one bin, or one zone. Set a timer and when it dings, you're done. You can always keep going if the vibe is right. But there's no pressure to go beyond the 10 minutes.
HIGH ENERGY	Time for a zone overhaul! Maybe it's your bathroom cabinets or your whole closet. You're in the zone, so use it! Put on a playlist that makes you feel like the main character and get after it, but don't overdo it. Which brings me to my second bonus tip.

Table 5: Entry point based on your current mental and physical state.

KNOW YOUR EFFORT BUDGET

Have you ever spent all your energy cleaning the pantry... and then had a meltdown because the dishes weren't done? Yeah, me too. That's why we need to talk about effort budgeting. Before you start a task, ask yourself: *How much gas is in my tank today?* Then, adjust your plans to match. Don't aim for productive hero. Focus on sustainable actions. Your time and energy are valuable. Spending less doesn't mean you're failing. It simply means you're being realistic and kind to your nervous system.

MOOD PAIRING

Mood pairing is when you choose to do a chore you hate, but you combine it with something you love. You pair the dreaded task with a sensory treat. Hate laundry? Watch your favorite YouTube series while you fold. Dread wiping the counters? Light a cozy candle or diffuse a scent you love. Need to sweep? Blast a soundtrack that makes you dance while you clean. It's like tricking your brain into a little bit of joy, getting the task done while also boosting your mood.

GRACE EXITS ARE ALLOWED

Sometimes, your brain just taps out mid-task. It's not sabotage, it's human. When this happens, I teach my clients the "grace exit." It's the art of walking away without feeling shame. Instead of spiraling into a *Why can't I finish anything*, try, *I got part of it done, and that's more than before.* Leave yourself a visual note or even set a reminder to return later. Your future self will thank you for saving some energy, but also for already getting started.

ENERGY BOOSTS

The final bonus tip to help with mood is to embrace an energy boost. When you're stuck in that "ugh" mode but want to keep moving, try one of these:

- Open a window for fresh air and sunlight.
- Do a cold water face splash.
- March in place or stretch for a minute.
- Change your outfit. Even swapping socks can help!

And if none of that works? Permission granted to rest! Rest is part of the process. You're not a machine; you're a human with a beautiful nonlinear brain, and you need rest.

CHAPTER TAKEAWAYS

01 Start with what you see. Visual clutter causes mental clutter. You don't have to finish everything, just clear one or two things from the coffee table.

---

02 Clean in dopamine-friendly layers and stop when your energy runs out. Remember to celebrate what you've accomplished, even if it's not everything you wanted to do.

---

03 Organize for real life and not for some fantasy you have.

---

04 Energy and mood matter more than motivation. Productivity isn't about willpower, but about knowing your effort budget and working with your brain.

---

05 Grace is part of the system, so stop if you need to. ADHD systems need to be flexible and forgiving.

PART

03

ROOM-BY-ROOM APPLICATION

"Successful people with ADHD are people who embrace distraction, not fight against it.

UNKNOWN

CHAPTER 5

A KITCHEN WITHOUT CHAOS

> In the midst of all the chaos swirling through your brain, all the disorganization and impulsiveness, the condition (ADHD) also seems to trigger a certain kind of creativity.
>
> DAVID NEELEMAN

The kitchen is often the place where I lose more than just my garlic press. I also lose my sanity. In fact, there was a time I nicknamed my kitchen "The War Zone." For many of my clients, this is the case, where the kitchen becomes somewhat of a Bermuda Triangle. You know, that magical place where Tupperware lids disappear, groceries expire in plain sight, and every drawer contains at least one mystery item that might be a broken appliance part.... or a tiny spaceship. It's hard to say.

For many ADHDers, the kitchen is the most-used, most-overwhelming space in the house. It's where we start and end our day, try to feed ourselves, maybe attempt a grown-up meal once in a while, and where the clutter tends to pile up fast. Why? Because kitchens require constant micro-decisions, which (if you've read earlier chapters) you now know can trigger decision fatigue and time blindness. That's why we often freeze in the kitchen and ask ourselves, *What am I doing here again?*

But there's good news: A chaotic kitchen isn't a personal failing. It's usually a sign that the space isn't working with your brain. And spoiler alert? Most traditional kitchen organizing advice assumes you're already operating with executive superpowers, which... yeah, no thank you. That's why this chapter is important. It's all about building a kitchen that helps you function, not frustrate you. In this chapter, we're going to:

- figure out where your high-use zones are so you stop walking back and forth like a confused raccoon
- declutter by function, not guilt or aesthetic pressure
- create batch-friendly systems for cleaning and meal prep
- harness the power of visibility and accessibility so food stops rotting and tools stop vanishing

Whether your kitchen is the size of a closet or a culinary castle, we're going to tame the chaos, one ADHD-proof trick at a time. Say goodbye to food that looks like a science experiment, long forgotten in the back of your fridge, and say hello to a slightly unconventional set-up that will work for you. Let's go find you a kitchen that allows you to eat, clean, and breathe.

HIGH-USE ZONES

Here's a game-changing idea: What if, instead of organizing your kitchen around what it should look like, you organize it around how you use it? I remember when I moved into my own apartment, I organized my kitchen the same way my mother organized hers, and her mother before that. Everything had a place. However, while my mother never seemed to struggle to keep things in place, my kitchen was all over the place! It was only much later, when I realized the kitchen layout police wasn't going to come after me, that I felt free to rearrange my kitchen as I wanted to.

When I started paying attention to my kitchen habits (and those of my clients), I realized that most clutter and frustration happen in the same 3–4 areas. These are called "high-use zones," and they are the places where we naturally gravitate to brew coffee, drop dishes, slice cheese sticks, or dig for snacks at 10 p.m. So, before you start rearranging everything or ordering 17 matching containers from Amazon, take a breath and do this instead.

Start by observing your kitchen habits. For the next few days, focus on noticing the following:

- Where do things always pile up?
- What's the first spot you touch when you walk into the kitchen?
- Where do you make your food versus where you wish you did?
- What do your kids/partner/roommates constantly drop or use?

Think of this like an anthropological study. But the subject is you, and the jungle is your countertop. Here are the most common high-use zones.

COFFEE AND TEA STATION

This one's sacred. If you're like me, your morning ritual lives here. To avoid a cluttering of spaces, create a designated area for coffee and tea. Set up everything in one place: mugs, pods, spoons, sweetener, even a trash bin if spills happen often (no shame here). Bonus points for a mini tray or basket to visually contain the chaos (Tuckman, 2017).

DISH DROP AND WASHING ZONE

This is usually the sink area—and it's often ground zero for overwhelm. Try a dish rack that matches your ADHD brain: simple, open, easy to unload. Put dish soap, scrubbers, and a towel within arm's reach. If you can't finish the whole sink, doing five minutes in this zone still counts.

FOOD PREP AREA

You know where you're always chopping veggies or assembling PB&Js? That's your prep zone. Keep your most frequently used tools nearby, such as the cutting board, knife, and trash bowl. I even recommend keeping a small bin under the counter for compost or quick wipe-downs. It's not fancy—it just works.

SNACK ZONE

I used to get so frustrated with my husband and my daughter because of their snacking habits. After school or work, they would drag snacks from the cupboard to the kitchen island I was trying to keep tidy and would sit there and indulge like sugar-fueled nomads. But then I stopped fighting it. Instead, I created a dedicated snack zone right there with a small bin, pre-portioned snacks, and napkins. No more crumbs everywhere. Just easy access and fewer battles.

These zones are behavioral anchors. They reflect your real habits and give you obvious, friction-free targets for tidying and improvement. They also give your brain a break: You don't have to make a million micro-decisions if your systems match your routines (Kooij et al., 2010). Let's make this practical: Grab a notebook or open your notes app on your phone and answer these questions:

1. What are the top three things you do in your kitchen daily?
2. Where do they happen most often?
3. What small change would make that task easier?

Remember, your goal isn't to change your behavior but to build around it. If the blender lives on the counter because you use it daily, make it its home. We're not staging a catalog, we're staging a life that works.

DECLUTTER BY FUNCTION

Okay, I'm going to say something super scandalous right now (don't tell The Home Edit). Sorting by category doesn't always work for ADHD brains. There. I said it. If you've ever tried the classic "put all like items together" rule and wound up with three overflowing drawers of spatulas and zero spoons when you need one, you're not alone. I used to be that person who had every ladle, lemon zester, and turkey baster in one drawer. Technically organized but functionally useless. That's because ADHD-friendly organizing works better when we group function, not just by item type. Think of it this way: Your brain doesn't say, "I need a whisk." It says, "I'm making pancakes, and I need all the pancake stuff." Your kitchen should reflect that logic, not fight it.

That's why we need to ask ourselves the magic question: What job does this space do? Instead of asking, *Where does this bowl live?* try asking yourself:

Once you've identified the job, clear the clutter that doesn't serve that job. By following this method, I've identified three functional zones in my kitchen:

THE KID LUNCH ZONE

If you want your children to be a little more involved and independent, I highly recommend having them pack their own lunches. To avoid chaos, give them one drawer with one rule: If it's not a lunch-packing tool, it doesn't go in here. When my daughter was still in school, the lunch zone drawer contained bento boxes, plastic forks and spoons, reusable snack bags, and a Sharpie for writing aggressive sandwich notes like "Eat me!"

THE BEFORE 9 A.M. SHELF

This shelf holds everything I touch in the early hours. It contains my coffee, protein bars, vitamins, and one emergency chocolate. It's my morning autopilot shelf, so I'm not mentally hiking Mount Decision at 7 a.m.

THE BAKING HAPPENS HERE CUPBOARD

I don't bake often, but when I do, I do it all at once. I corralled all my baking supplies—measuring cups, mixing bowls, cake pans, sprinkles, the works—into one lower cupboard. Now, I don't have to hunt for a cupcake tin like I'm on a scavenger hunt with bad lighting.

It's your turn for a functional declutter. Don't worry, you're not alone. Start by writing down or saying the answers out loud to the following decluttering prompts.

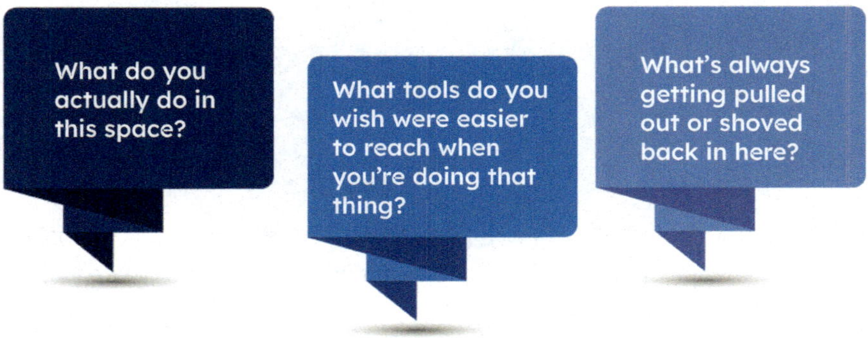

Once you've answered these questions, start decluttering only the items that interfere with that function. Even if that means the third immersion blender finally goes in the donation bin. Remember, you're not a chef in a restaurant. You're a human in a house with a real brain, real needs, and probably a pile of receipts somewhere. If sorting by function makes you feel smoother, do that. Always pick what works over what looks good on organizing shows.

BATCH-CLEAN AND MEAL PREP

Let's be real. For many ADHDers, cleaning the kitchen and cooking meals can feel like trying to herd feral cats while someone yells obscure baking instructions in your ear. It's not that we can't do it, but that by the time we get the motivation, the mess has multiplied, the energy has left the building, and dinner is... cereal? This section isn't about becoming a meal-prepping, stainless-steel-countertop god or goddess. It's about finding realistic loops and simple food systems that work even when your executive function is playing hide and seek. Are you ready to dive in? Let's do this!

THE CLEAN LOOP

The ADHD brain thrives on momentum, but here's the thing about momentum: It dies. If you don't know where to start or how to keep it going, momentum can die out faster than it started. This is where the clean-up loop comes into play. The clean-up loop isn't a deep clean. It's a rinse and reset. And it can be done in less time than it takes to scroll three reels of cats knocking stuff off tables. Here's how it works:

01 Begin with the trash. Use it as a quick win to build motivation. Simply get rid of anything that is, well, trash.

02 Next up, we're tackling the dishes. Don't worry, we're not going all perfection here. We're going for better, not better than anyone else.

03 Now, it's time to wipe the counters, stovetop, and maybe a splatter on the fridge that's been there since last Tuesday. Again, doesn't have to be perfect, just clean enough.

04 And now you're done. That's all. Step away before your brain starts suggesting you scrub the grout.

This loop will take between 5 and 15 minutes, and it's all you need to reset your kitchen. To make it fun, choose a song you like or set a visible timer and see how much you can get done within that timeframe.

MEAL PREPPING FOR REAL LIFE

Now that the kitchen looks vaguely human again, let's talk about feeding yourself without burning out. ADHD meal prep isn't about pre-cooking 17 casseroles in matching containers. It's about reducing the number of decisions you have to make between 4 and 7 p.m. Here are some ADHD brain-friendly strategies you can try:

The Three-Ingredient Dinner

If a recipe calls for more than three ingredients and steps, my brain immediately goes on strike. So, here's what I aim for:

- Protein plus veggies plus a shortcut. For example, a rotisserie chicken, a bag salad, and some naan bread.
- One-pan meals, where you can literally throw everything together in one pan.
- Stir-fry kits or frozen pre-made meals. The less mental math I have to do, the better.

Will these recipes earn me a Michelin star? Of course not. But it will fill my family's belly.

Build-Your-Own Night

Also known as "lazy genius magic." On a build-your-own night, everyone jumps in to create their own plate of food. All you have to do is place all the ingredients on the table. Whether it's tacos, sandwiches, or wraps, everyone will take charge of their plate, which means less stress for you. Everyone will get their food. There will be no complaints. And you'll have five minutes to breathe instead of cooking for everyone. You can also modify this as much as you want. Whatever can be assembled at the table means less stress for you.

Protein and Snack Bins

ADHDers often forget to eat, or they forget they have already eaten and then panic-eat a slice of toast at 2 p.m. Why not make it easier on yourself by prepping bins you can grab and go from? A protein bin might contain things like yogurt, deli meat, pre-cooked chicken, or cheese sticks. A snack bin might include nuts, bars, fruit, and hummus. However, it's super important to store these bins at eye level so you can see them and use them. It should serve as a reminder, not need reminding of.

Veggies That Don't Need Therapy First

I know those spiraled zucchinis and onion flowers look beautiful, but let's not pretend we'll have time (or the mental capacity) to make them or use them in a way that brings them justice. Skip the fluff and go for the veggies that are accessible and not intimidating. Get the baby carrots and the bag of pre-cut and washed broccoli florets. Better yet, grab the veggies you can pop in the microwave! If you have veggies that aren't more admin than cooking a Sunday roast, you're more likely to eat them.

One of my clients, Lucy, realized that Monday nights were always chaotic. It overwhelmed her to think about cooking meals everyone would enjoy, so she needed a smart, ADHD-friendly plan to remove some of the pressure. Introducing Picnic Night. Instead of trying to fight the chaos and prepare a three-course meal, she leaned into it. Every Monday night, she grabs a picnic basket and fills it with all the snacks she can find. It might be leftovers from the weekend, fruits, cheese, crackers, or even raw veggies. Then, her children take turns choosing the picnic spot in their house. Whether it's in front of the TV, under the dining table, or outside, they have a picnic night. Lucy doesn't have to cook or pretend like the day isn't chaotic, and the kids absolutely love it! On top of that, it's a great way to spend time together as a family.

At the end of the day, it doesn't matter what you eat or how you clean. What matters is that you find ways to honor your energy, attention, and time. If batch-cleaning helps you feel a little less overwhelmed and meals are slightly easier to manage? It's a win.

POWER OF VISIBILITY AND ACCESSIBILITY

You've heard me say a few times already that we need to prioritize function over aesthetics. The same is very much true when it comes to your kitchen. The prettiest pantry isn't always the most helpful. In fact, take a moment right now and remove any of the pressure you might feel to create a picture-perfect pantry. Whether it's pressure you put on yourself or something someone said many years ago, let it go. Release the pressure and accept that your pantry needs to be different.

If your flour is in a beautiful, matching, airtight jar but your brain forgets it exists, then guess what? You'll still buy more flour next week. You'll open the cabinet, stare into the abyss, and say, "We have nothing to eat." Pretty is nice, there's no denying that, but visible is functional, which is so much better. ADHD brains take the "out of sight, out of mind" very literally.

> When it comes to storage, the best system is the one you can see, reach, and remember.

OPEN BINS ARE NOT A MORAL FAILING

Despite what some organization shows might say, open bins are not the enemy. Open bins, plastic baskets, and lazy Susans (the kitchen tool, not your neighbor) are the unsung heroes of ADHD-friendly kitchens. Because you know what none of them require? Memory. Here are three things I suggest every ADHD-friendly kitchen needs:

- Shelf risers: These handy tools will make everything in the cupboard visible, not just the front row.
- Turntables: Turntables bring sauces out of hiding like a smart magic trick. I have multiple turntables in my fridge and pantry to make all my ingredients accessible and visible.
- Fridge drawer labels: This might sound funny, but labeling your fridge is a great way to keep track of what you have and what goes where inside the fridge. When you have the drawers labeled, you are more likely to check them and not forget about the two-week-old lettuce that's turning gray.

The more you can see, the more likely you are to use what you have. Visibility reduces food waste, repeated purchases, and that deep sigh of "Ugh, why do I do this?"

Little confession time: There was a point in my life when I found three separate containers of identical leftover pasta in the fridge. They were moldy, forgotten, and hiding behind a salad kit that never had a chance. So, I started a new system in my fridge. One of the drawers I labeled "Eat First." It's the first drawer you see when you open the fridge, and in there, I know to put everything that's going to expire first. Not only does it help me, but my family also knows to grab from that drawer first. It's not fancy, but it works.

WALL-MOUNTED RACKS

Have you ever struggled with the "I forgot I had that" syndrome? Same. This happens often with kitchen tools. Here's the thing: If your can opener, measuring cups, or spatula is buried under a drawer full of twist ties and rogue batteries, chances are you're going to avoid cooking entirely. Instead, mount it. Hang it. Clip it. Display it.

- Install hooks inside your cabinet doors to hang some of the bigger utensils you use often.
- Use wall-mounted magnetic strips for knives and other tools you want handy.
- Put stove hooks on the backsplash for measuring spoons or oven mits.
- Even a simple over-the-door shoe organizer can become a snack or seasoning rack.

It's not clutter. It's accessibility. And when everything has a place to hang or be mounted, you are more likely to return the item to that place. Remember, the goal of an ADHD-friendly kitchen is to reduce friction, not add to it. Your kitchen doesn't have to look like a magazine cover—it's there to nourish, comfort, and work for you.

CHAPTER TAKEAWAYS

01 Your kitchen doesn't have to make sense to anyone but you. Identify your high-use zones based on how you and your people use the space, not how you think you should.

02 Decluttering by function instead of putting it all together is an ADHD power move. Your brain loves context, and it will help you to remember where things go.

03 Batch cleaning and meal prep work best in snackable chunks. Use timers, loops, and music to keep things doable and perhaps even enjoyable.

04 Visibility is more powerful than pretty. Clear bins, open baskets, and turntables will help you to see what you have, saving time, money, and your last nerve.

05 A kitchen that works for your brain is the best kind of kitchen. It's not about creating a showroom but having a space where you can feed yourself with less friction and more success.

CHAPTER 6

CLOSETS, CLOTHES, AND DECISION FATIGUE

> You don't learn to walk by following rules. You learn by doing, and by falling over
>
> RICHARD BRANSON

If you've ever stood in front of your closet, half-dressed, mildly sweaty, already late, and thought, *I have nothing to wear,* while staring at three overstuffed hangers and a chair-drobe… you're in the right place. Clothes are personal. They're more than fabric. They're memory, mood, identity, aspiration, comfort, and sometimes guilt. They might be jammed into drawers we can't close, but they mean more to the ADHD mind than just clothing. For ADHDers, the relationship with clothing is rarely just about style. It's about feeling like ourselves while also not getting derailed by zippers, tags, or an avalanche of "someday" pants.

This chapter is where we ditch the pressure to have a curated capsule wardrobe or a YouTube-perfect closet. Instead, we're going to get honest about what's wearable, what's causing mental clutter, and how to make your wardrobe work for your brain instead of against it. We'll talk about how ADHDers often wrestle with identity through clothes (hello, three abandoned fashion eras), how decision fatigue turns morning outfits into full-blown quests, and why embracing a type of uniform might feel freeing and not like a fashion sentence. And yes, we'll also talk about the pile… You know the one.

So, grab your comfiest sweatpants, the hoodie with mystery stains, and maybe a laundry basket that hasn't seen action in days because this chapter is about to help you make peace with your clothes, one guilt-free step at a time. Ready? Let's open the closet and exhale. No shame, just solutions.

THE POWER OF CLOTHES AND IDENTITY

For the average person, closets hold clothes. For ADHDers? Closets hold selves. Plural. Former selves, fantasy selves, hopeful selves, and yes, sometimes forgotten selves. That sequin top? That's from your "maybe I'm a karaoke queen" era. The navy blue blazer? That's corporate-you who had his life together and drank Americanos like a grown-up. Not to mention the workout tank tops that still whisper, "One day, we'll start that Couch to 5K workout plan. Maybe."

ADHD brains are deeply tied to emotion and narrative, which means clothing doesn't just serve a functional purpose; it carries stories (Matlen, 2017). A shirt isn't just a shirt. It's "the one I wore on that vacation before my life fell apart." A pair of shoes? "These were for interviews I never went to, but still meant something." Even clothes that don't fit can feel too loaded to toss. Letting go of items can feel like deleting a version of yourself.

Take my client Jenna. Her closet had three main categories: law school Jenna (blazers and sensible shoes), toddler-mom Jenna (yoga pants, snack crumbs included), and fantasy fitness Jenna (a whole bunch of untouched sports bras and matching sets). The funny part? She was currently working from home in tech, living in hoodies and jeans. Yet, every time she opened her closet, she felt paralyzed. Why? Because each section was a visual *should*. A reminder of what she'd left behind or hadn't become yet.

Keeping identity-tied clothing doesn't mean you're weak or overly sentimental. It means you're human, especially if you have ADHD. We feel deeply, we remember flashes, and we hold onto potential like it's currency (Hallowell & Ratey, 2021). But here's where I gently nudge: Your closet is not a museum. You don't need a whole exhibit for every life chapter.

What helped Jenna (and me) was to reframe clothing not as proof of success or failure, but as tools for the present.

> If something doesn't support the version of you you're trying to care for today, it's okay to let it go.

That doesn't erase who you were or who you dreamed of being. In fact, keeping one item from a past chapter (a scarf, a tee, a memory jacket) can feel more meaningful than hoarding the entire collection. For example, I kept a soft red blazer from my varsity days. Not because I'll wear it in my current career or stage of life, but because it reminds me of the strong young woman I became during those years. And that's enough reason for me to feel inspired.

So, here's your personal invitation: As you look through your closet, instead of asking, "Does this fit?" ask this instead: "Does this support who I am right now?" Let the pieces that no longer do quietly retire, with thanks. You're not giving up, you're making space. Take a moment to reflect on the following prompts before we move on to the next section:

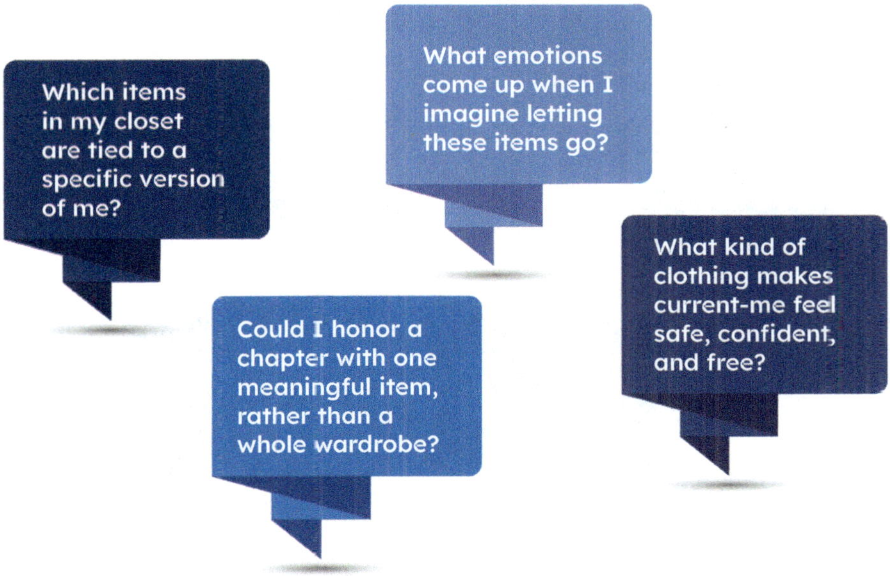

CLOTHING CHOICE PARALYSIS

If you've ever stood in front of your closet at 8:07 a.m., half-dressed, staring into the abyss of hangers while internally screaming because none of your 43 shirts feel right, you're not alone, and you're not insane. You've just been confronted with clothing choice paralysis, ADHD edition. As much as the ADHD brain loves novelty and keeping things interesting, it doesn't love a buffet of options. We think we do, because choices sound like fun, but then we get hit with the real cost: decision fatigue. And when it's first thing in the morning, when our executive function is still stretching and yawning, that closet chaos can derail the whole day.

Here's why: Every shirt isn't just a shirt. It's a decision. It's a mini math equation of weather, mood, body image, comfort level, upcoming task, and what's clean (or at least doesn't smell too suspicious). Now multiply that by pants, socks, shoes, layers, and boom. You have a short circuit. What many ADHDers don't realize is that the problem isn't your clothes. It's the volume of micro-decisions you're being forced to make at your most vulnerable moment. The real friction point isn't just "I don't know what to wear," it's "This process makes me feel behind before I've even started." So, let's cut down the friction, shall we?

To get started, ask yourself:

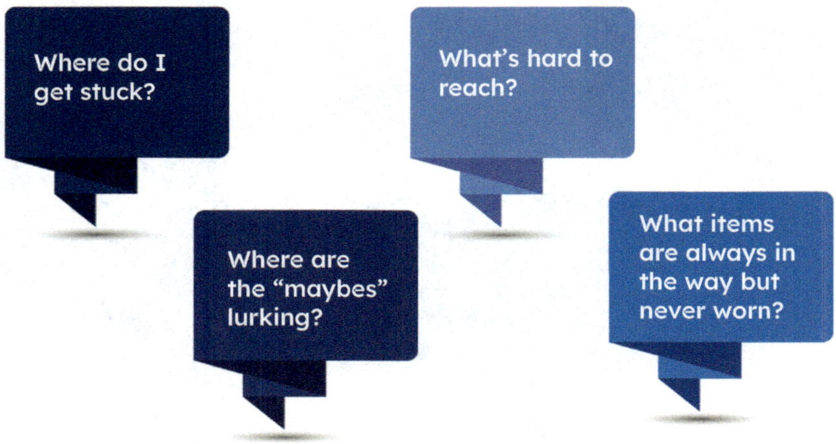

A lot of ADHDers hang on to clothing "just in case." You know, just in case you go to that one event, just in case it fits next month, just in case you finally figure out how to style it. But maybe clothes are clutter that whispers doubt before you've even picked your favorite pair of socks. So, what can we do about it? We need to create a system. Here are a few of my favorite methods that I (and many of my clients) swear by:

- **The three-category sort:** Separate your clothes into "Home," "Outside," and "Special." It doesn't have to be fancy. A simple labeled drawer, a trio of color-coded hangers, or even a Sharpie-marked tag can work. The goal? Make what you need now easy to see, grab, and wear.
- **The weekly rack:** Every Sunday (or whatever day of the week you want to use), pre-select your outfits for the week. It's like meal prepping, but for your clothes. You can use a rolling rack, a shelf, or even hang five hangers on the back of your door. That's five days of decision-free dressing.
- **Capsule collection:** Capsule wardrobes have been all the rage the last couple of years. While they seem great in principle, it can get a little boring. If you're not familiar, a capsule wardrobe is where you seriously edit your closet and keep only a few basics. The idea is that every item in your closet should work with every item in your closet, removing any clashing. This often means having only neutral colors or sticking to very basic items. While it can be beneficial, it can also get boring quickly. So, instead of creating one capsule wardrobe, create a few capsule collections. Build mini wardrobes with mix-and-match pieces that fit your lifestyle. You can rotate these mini wardrobes seasonally or by mood, reducing choice, not style.
- **Limit hangers:** Give yourself a hanger cap. If it doesn't fit in the space, something's got to go. This helps with those "but what if I need this for a party" hoarding instincts.

When you streamline your clothing choices, you're not being boring. You're creating breathing room. The goal isn't to have a closet that could grace a lifestyle magazine. The goal is to get dressed in under five minutes without having a meltdown. And if all else fails? Remember that no one ever died from wearing the same hoodie three days in a row.

BUILDING A FREEING UNIFORM

Let's play a quick word association game: I say "uniform," you say...

Boring? Restrictive? Trauma from middle school dress codes?

Well, what if it doesn't have to be that way? What if uniform was synonymous with freedom, excitement, and comfort? In the ADHD world, a uniform isn't about giving up style and individuality. It's about giving up the daily brain battle. A uniform is a shortcut, not a sentence. It's you saying, "Let's take one thing off the mental plate so I can use my limited executive function for something else. Like eating breakfast. Or finding my car keys." Why do uniforms work for the ADHD brain?

Uniforms eliminate a hundred little decisions before your brain has had caffeine. You don't have to decide how things fit together, or whether that one weird sleeve works with your jacket, or if those pants require ironing (spoiler: they usually do, and we both know you're not going to do it). By pre-deciding what your default outfit is, you're giving your future self a giant break. In fact, research supports that reducing decision points early in the day can help preserve executive function for higher-stakes tasks later on (Parker & Boutelle, 2009). The fewer things we have to choose, the more gas we save in the tank.

THE RIGHT FORMULA

Now, a uniform doesn't mean a literal uniform. It's more of a formula that you've tried, tested, and loved. It's a recipe you use to create outfits every day to remove any stress or surprise outfits that don't work together. To find the right formula for yourself, begin by asking the following questions:

- *What outfit makes me feel both comfy and semi-human?*
- *Which pieces do I reach for even when everything else is clean?*
- *What's my go-to when I have five minutes and no patience?*

Your uniform might be:

- black leggings + oversized tee + cardigan
- jean + graphic tee + hoodie
- joggers + tank + zip-up
- comfy dress + stretchy bike shorts underneath
- button-down shirt + comfy chino pants + fun sneakers

If it feels too restricting, remember that you don't have to commit to one single look forever. Think of the uniform as a template—a plug-and-play combo you can dress up, dress down, or accessorize depending on the mood or occasion.

MAKE IT EASY

Once you've identified your top-tier clothes, make them ridiculously easy to access. I call this your "go-to zone." You could do this by having a dedicated drawer for your uniform pieces or stacking them at eye level in your closet. You can also use labeled bins or hanging organizers by category. In my own life, I have a little cubby labeled "Outfits that work when I'm over it." Inside are three versions of the same black T-shirt, a handful of stretchy pants, and a denim jacket that makes everything feel put together. I accessorize these based on my mood and know I'll feel comfortable. Will I be voted most stylish person of the day? Nope. But will I have a mental breakdown because I couldn't find something to wear? Also no, which is a win.

Here's the best part: A uniform isn't the death of your personality. It's the foundation for self-expression. You can still rotate accessories, rock rainbow socks, or add a fun hat on a Tuesday if the mood strikes. The point is, you're starting from a base that already works. Think of it like building a burrito bowl. The rice and beans are the uniform, and you get to play with the toppings. Uniforms aren't about shrinking yourself into sameness. They're about making consistent wins easier. When you free up your morning brainpower, you're more likely to leave the house on time, feel good in your body, and maybe even remember your water bottle.

EMBRACE THE PILE

Let's talk about *the pile*... (insert dramatic music and mysterious fog). Just kidding. I know the pile might seem like an evil villain or a monster you need to defeat, but like most "bad guys," the pile is just misunderstood. Take a moment to identify your pile: Is it on a chair? Perhaps next to the laundry basket? Maybe it's on your wardrobe floor? Well, the pile can be part memory archive, part soft mountain of denial, but it's also totally normal. The pile is very rarely born out of laziness. It's simply decision fatigue in fabric form.

Instead of fighting the pile, let's befriend it. Let's turn it into something that helps us figure out what to wear and what to keep without sending us into a shame spiral that lasts a week. That's why I stand by the three-pile method. Forget those hyper-speed decluttering montages where everything gets folded into tiny rectangles by people who definitely don't have executive functioning challenges. We're going for clarity, not perfection. So, here's how the three-pile system works:

PILE 1
KEEP IN SIGHT

PILE 2
TRY AGAIN LATER

PILE 3
OUT YOU GO

PILE 1: KEEP IN SIGHT

This is the "good stuff" pile. It's the pile with the clothes you can't bear to go without. They include all the items that:

- feel good right now
- fit your body as it is
- get worn at least once a week
- make you do a little internal happy dance

These clothes go front and center on a shelf, hanger, or in a bin you see and reach for every day. It needs to be visible and usable. If you can't see it—RIP to that cute outfit.

PILE 2: TRY AGAIN LATER

The second pile is the maybe pile, and it deserves a loving middle ground. These items get bagged, binned, or boxed with a 30-day label. You're not deciding right now. You're simply deferring strategically. Maybe if you're unsure whether that jacket is still your style or if you're not sure if you want to be a blazer person again, then put it in the "try again later" pile. Maybe you're just not emotionally ready to say goodbye to that shirt you brought for a date that never happened, and that's okay. Give it 30 days. Put it in a pile box, add a label, and set a reminder to come back to it in 30 days. When the time comes, open it with fresh eyes and far less pressure.

PILE 3: OUT YOU GO

The last pile is the "please leave" pile. It's the items that no longer serve your current self. Even if it's items you've never worn or the jeans you've been hoping to fit into... It's time to say bye-bye. You might not know it, but they're probably whispering some bad things about you, telling you that there's something wrong with your body or style choices. But it's time to set them free and ask them to leave. Give yourself permission to donate things you "should" love but never wear, release items tied to an outdated version of yourself, and say thank you and goodbye without folding them into origami first. And just in case you need a reminder:

> Letting go of the clothes doesn't mean you're letting go of the dream. You're just making room for new dreams... one that involves less laundry limbo.

While making these three piles, don't push yourself into a state of burnout. Instead, use this checklist to keep you on track:

1. Set a 20-minute timer.
2. Pick one drawer, shelf, or chair pile to sort.
3. Use the three-pile system.
4. Stop when the timer ends (seriously).
5. Reward yourself.

If you don't finish everything today, that's also okay. You made progress, and that's a win.

CHAPTER TAKEAWAYS

01 Your closet might be housing versions of you from different chapters of life. That's not clutter—it's emotional history.

02 Staring down a chaotic closet first thing in the morning can short-circuit your brain. Minimize friction by curating outfits that are visible and accessible.

03 Creating your go-to outfit formula isn't boring; it's liberating. Your brain gets more energy for life's actual demands, like answering emails or remembering where your phone is.

04 Use the three-pile system to identify which items work for you and release those that no longer serve you.

05 Progress isn't perfection, and that's okay. Start with one item at a time.

CHAPTER 7

LIVING ROOMS, WORK AREAS, AND DROP ZONES

> As soon as something stops being fun, I think it's time to move on. Life is too short to be unhappy.
>
> RICHARD BRANSON

If we're being honest, in an ADHD household, the living room is never just a living room. It's also home to the craft table, the office, the late-night snack zone, the laundry station, the napping cave, and the unofficial lost-and-found of the entire house. That corner chair? It hasn't been sat in since last August because it's currently housing five sweaters, two Amazon boxes, and a dog leash you swear you returned to the basket. If this is the reality you live in, that's okay. Just like all roads lead to Rome, all clutter tends to lead to the living room. But here's something you might not know:

> A messy living room doesn't mean you're broken—it means your system is.

Most neurotypical organizing advice treats these overlapping roles as problems to be solved. They suggest having only "living room" activities in the living room. But you and I both know you're going to haul that laundry from the other side of the house toward the comfy couch anyway. So, why fight it? In an ADHD home, we're not trying to turn you into someone else. We're designing for how you actually live. Think of it as organized clutter. But that means we need to acknowledge your need for visibility, your tendency to drop things the second you walk in, and your very real desire to have a functional space without sacrificing your ability to breathe, think, or locate your earbuds.

This chapter is all about creating small wins in your most-used zones, especially the ones that tend to become clutter hotspots. We'll set up drop zones that don't turn into doom piles, build workspaces that won't eat your sanity, and reduce visual chaos without stuffing everything into a cabinet you'll forget exists in five minutes. So, grab your coziest blanket (yes, the one from the floor), toss the remote somewhere reasonable, and let's start turning your "all-the-things" areas into "just-enough-things" spaces.

HOW VISIBILITY AIDS MEMORY

One of ADHD's sneakiest tricks is object permanence issues. For those of us with ADHD, the old saying "Out of sight, out of mind" isn't just a proverb about relationships but a lifestyle hazard. If we don't see it, it might as well never have existed. That's why you can't find the remote even though it's on the couch (under the pillow), and it's also why your tax papers are still MIA despite being "put in a safe place." Have you ever put something away for safekeeping and thought to yourself, *Wow, what a great and safe place to put this*, only to immediately forget where that safe space is? Like, you can remember you put it somewhere for safekeeping, but you can't remember where? That's object permanence at its best.

The ADHD brain is wired to value visibility because it is more engaging than relying on verbal cues or memory alone. So, when something gets tucked away, whether into a drawer, behind a cabinet door, or under a well-meaning organizational bin with a lid, it becomes invisible. And invisible things don't get remembered. Or used. Or found again until next spring cleaning madness. Now, this doesn't mean you're doomed to live in a see-through jungle of bins and baskets. But it does mean we should focus on storage solutions that work with your brain and not against it. Let's break it down:

VISIBILITY EQUALS MEMORY BOOST

If you want to stop losing your keys, headphones, wallet, and sanity, you have to make them visually available (maybe not the sanity part, though). A client of mine, Pedro, used to lose his keys all the time. It got so bad that he decided to never take his keys off the lanyard around his neck. You know what happened? He would "misplace" his keys, look for them for 20 minutes, and then realize they had been around his neck the whole time. While the lanyard was with him, it wasn't visible unless he looked in a mirror. Open baskets, wall-mounted hooks, and clear containers by the door are great and easy ways to boost memory, allowing you to see where your things are.

I used to lose my headphones daily. I'm not kidding—daily. I'd waste so much time retracing my steps, swearing they were right there, and then melting into a puddle of frustration. The solution? A simple hook on the side of my computer screen. It's visible, it's easy to reach, and it's right where I need my headphones the most. The best part? I haven't lost them since.

VISUAL CLUTTER VS. FUNCTIONAL VISIBILITY

Now, I know what you're thinking: *Amy, aren't you always telling us to reduce clutter? Won't open storage make my space look messy?* To that I say, "It might." But visibility and clutter aren't the same things, especially when your visual items are intentional. The difference is in the purpose. That leaning tower of unread mail? Mental noise. A clear acrylic file rack with a labeled folder you actually check? Mentally supportive. Both are visible. Neither is shoved into a cupboard. But one is functional, and the other is leading toward a visual avalanche. Here are a few ways you can keep something visual, without making it feel cluttered:

- open shelving for frequently used items like remotes or journals
- wall hooks for bags, keys, or headphones
- transparent storage bins for cords, tech, or seasonal stuff you want to remember exists
- visible labels that actually make sense to your brain (Think "mail to open" instead of "papers.")
- drop trays or baskets in living room hot spots for items that rotate in and out

It's all about keeping the right things in sight, but not everything. Your brain doesn't want more stuff; it wants more clarity. So, next time you find yourself spiraling over the "Where did I put..." mystery, remember that it's not about forgetfulness, but about visibility. And visibility is a tool you can use.

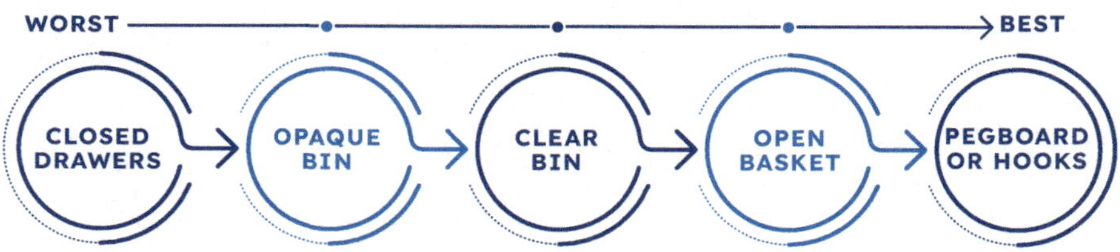

CREATING A DROP ZONE

If I could install just one system in every ADHD household across the world, it would be the drop zone. No, it's not a theme park ride, even though ADHD often feels like a roller coaster. It's a simple, powerful, life-saving space that stops the morning scramble in its tracks. It's also a tool I've already mentioned in this book, but now it's time to really dig into it. An effective drop zone allows you to keep track of everyday items like bags, keys, sunglasses, wallets, permission slips, and charging cables. So, what exactly is it?

A drop zone is a designated, clearly labeled area, ideally right where you come in and out of the house, where the essentials tend to land anyway. No thinking. No wandering. Just muscle memory meets mental relief. The ADHD brain thrives on external structure, and that's exactly what the drop zone offers. It reduces decision fatigue, prevents the endless "Where did I put it" loop, and makes your future self want to high-five present you. But a drop zone is more than just a "dumping ground." While you don't need a fancy mudroom or Pinterest-worthy entryway, you do need a few essentials to ensure the drop zone is effective.

- **Hook:** Your drop zone needs a hook that can be used for keys, bags, hats, dog leashes, or whatever tends to vanish right when you need it most. Wall hooks are easy to install and can be as cute or boring as your heart desires.

- **Bowl or tray:** Your drop zone needs a bowl or tray to catch things like sunglasses, earbuds, loose change, random hair ties, or that LEGO piece your kid swore was important. Choose something shallow and hard to ignore. Don't pick a bowl that's too deep or opaque, as it will become a vacuum.
- **File or magazine rack:** This is for important papers like mail, forms, permission slips, and receipts. Label each slot with a clear instruction, like "To read," "To sign," or "To shred."
- **Labels:** Even if it feels obvious, your brain needs a visual cue to remember to use the drop zone. Labels will also help rewire habit loops, especially when everyone in the house is using the same space.

One of my clients, Gregory, urgently needed a drop zone. After three consecutive days of lost lunchboxes, he gathered his three children and said, "We're building a station so your stuff doesn't evaporate into the void." They picked a small wall near the front door, and each kid got a wall-mounted basket with their name on it. Below that, there was a bowl for keys, a labeled mail rack, and even a Command strip hook for car keys. Within a week, the morning chaos went from hurricane to a mild breeze. Did it stay perfectly tidy? No. But did it stop the early morning screams of "Where are your lunch boxes?!" You bet.

SETTING UP THE DROP ZONE

Now, let's look at how you can practically incorporate a drop zone into your home. Remember to have fun with it and make it your own!

1. **Pick the place:** Begin by choosing a spot where you naturally dump your things. It's probably not a closet or a room on the other side of the house. It's most likely a surface near the door or a kitchen counter that is already getting overworked.

2. **Start with what you own:** Use items you already have to create the drop zone. It's not necessary to go out and spend money on it. Instead, repurpose a cereal bowl or use an old magazine file. Fancy can come later. For now, focus on function and what you have.
3. **Label things:** The third step is to label every spot on the drop zone. Make it personal, but keep it clear so everyone can understand what goes where.
4. **Designate spots:** Make sure that every person in the house has a spot. This will avoid the "Whose junk is this?" debates and make maintenance more likely. It also adds some collaboration and teaches responsibility and accountability.
5. **Practice the habit:** You might have to repeat things out loud during the first few weeks. Say to yourself and your family, "Keys on the hook," as you enter the house. Yes, it might sound a little like a cartoon narrator, but it works, and it will help you build the muscle memory.

The key lies in making it yours. Don't be scared to personalize it or try something new. A drop zone isn't a one-size-fits-all system. If you have a pet, I recommend giving them a space on the wall, too. If you carry a planner with you, make sure there's a spot for it on the drop zone. Or, if you love sticky notes, turn the wall above into your new ADHD-friendly bulletin board. The goal is repetition. The more consistent the drop-off spot, the more friction we remove on a daily basis.

ADHD-FRIENDLY WORK ZONE

Now, let's talk home workspaces. Have you ever opened your laptop on the couch and then found yourself folding laundry, eating pretzels, and reorganizing the junk drawer 42 minutes later? If yes, you're in excellent company. ADHD brains need a very specific kind of environment to thrive. It might not be picture-perfect or minimalist, but it needs to be clear, fiction-free, and movement-tolerant. Your work zone should help you start, stick, and recenter, not stare blankly at your pens and spiral into decision fatigue. How can we create that? By using the ADHD work zone rulebook, which you're allowed to break at any time.

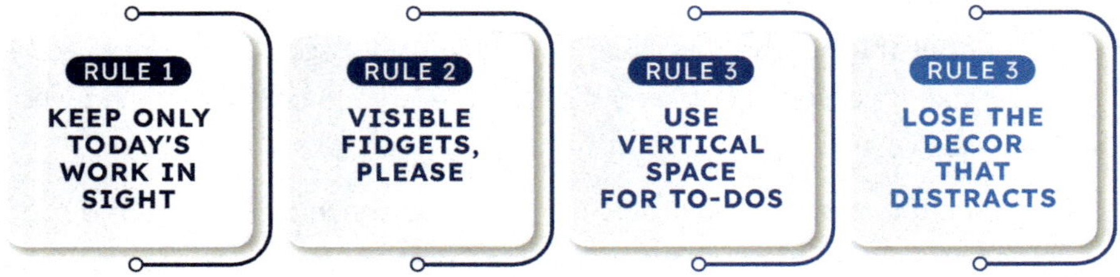

RULE 1: KEEP ONLY TODAY'S WORK IN SIGHT

That giant stack of papers labeled "someday" is lying to you. It's not motivating, and it's not a "reminder." It's a burden, and it's smothering your brain. ADHD brains are time-blind, so everything feels urgent, even when it's not due for another three weeks. The best way to avoid that unnecessary time pressure is by keeping one clipboard with the day's to-do list front and center. The rest? Hide it in labeled drawers or folders for tomorrow or the day after. As long as what you need to do today is visible, the rest can wait.

RULE 2: VISIBLE FIDGETS, PLEASE

It's a common misconception that fidgeting is a sign of not paying or a lack of focus. In reality, fidgeting helps regulate focus, not distract from it (Sharp, 2024). So, ditch the guilt and display your fidgets like a curated collection. Show off your sick stress ball collection, clicky pens, and chewable jewelry (yes, grown-ups can have these, too). I keep mine in a mesh basket right on the desk. If I don't see it, I won't use it, and then I'll just click my mouse aggressively until it breaks. It's better for me, and my mouse, to keep my fidget toys where I can see them.

RULE 3: USE VERTICAL SPACE FOR TO-DOS

What might seem like chaos to others can work for you and me. Sticky notes, for one, can work great if you have a set of rules to use them. I suggest using a small corkboard or wall grid to post just three visual reminders at a time. Instead of having a chaotic ocean of sticky notes everywhere, prioritize three notes at a time. This might include reminders like "Email Jen," "Pay water bill," or "Take meds." Keep them bite-sized and eye-level, or you'll start ignoring the wall altogether (you know, like that load of clean laundry that's been on the stairs for four days).

RULE 4: LOSE THE DECOR THAT DISTRACTS

I love a good inspirational quote, but if your home office has a dozen signs that say "You got this!" while your to-do list says "You absolutely do not got this," it might be time to take a different approach to decorating. While some decor can be fun and exciting to look at, others might cause more of a distraction than do good. Remember, the ADHD brain gets overstimulated easily, which is why it's crucial to remove anything from your workspace that doesn't add to focus or accomplishing the task (even if it is adorable).

With these four rules in mind, you can create the perfect office space that works for you. But here's the thing:

> You won't always have your own office or space. Sometimes, you might have to share a space or desperately seek an empty seat at home to get some work done.

Luckily, an ADHD working space doesn't necessarily require walls or a fancy desk. Even a small corner on the dining table or a spot on the floor can work.

If your "office" needs to be portable, here are a few things to keep in mind to make it work for your brain:

- Make it easy to move. Choose a portable cart or something with only the essentials to make it easy to pick up and work from wherever.
- Ensure that your portable office has all the necessities, like a planner, a clipboard, and a fidget toy.
- Use a tray to keep your items in the open so you don't forget where your "office" is.

My mobile system includes a small rolling cart with three tiers: the top for my laptop and daily planner, the middle for pens and sticky notes, and the bottom for other items like snacks, chargers, and a fidget toy. When I roll into a new space, it's like I'm mentally declaring that the zone is officially the focus zone.

REDUCING VISUAL STATIC WITHOUT HIDING EVERYTHING

Have you ever run into the little monster I like to call Visual Static? You know, that blur of stuff that your eyes scan over but your brain just screams "NOPE!" It's when every surface seems to be auditioning for a part in a clutter horror movie. Even if the items are technically organized, the visual chaos makes your ADHD brain slide right into avoidance mode. Not because you're lazy, but because too many visual inputs fry our attention circuits. Now, let me clarify:

> This is not a call to shove everything you see into a drawer and forget about it. Hiding everything isn't helpful, especially not in the long run. Instead, this is about shaping what's visible so your brain doesn't go into cognitive overload.

To reduce visual static, here are a few things you can try:

VISUAL ZONING: ORGANIZE BY USE, NOT JUST LOOKS

We spoke about this in a previous chapter, but it's crucial when it comes to workspaces as well. Group your items by behavioral clusters, not categories. This is what I call visual zoning. For example, if your couch is the hub for TV-watching, have a small bin on the side table with the remote, reading glasses, and perhaps another fidget toy. On the coffee table, you can have a tray with coasters, tissues, and other things that belong in the "hang out" zone. This gives your brain a visual roadmap instead of a *Where's Waldo* puzzle.

COLOR CLUSTERING: TRICK THE BRAIN INTO SEEING LESS

Color clustering is a little visual Jedi mind trick. When you group like-colored items, your brain sees fewer "units" of information, which makes it feel calmer. While some colorful items are good for differentiating between things, it's also advised to use the same color if things fall into the same category. For example, I swapped my rainbow bins for matching gray drawers, but I made the labels colorful. That way, it's less distracting to my brain, but it still allows me to find a place for everything.

TRAY CONTAINMENT: BECAUSE 5 THINGS CAN BECOME 1

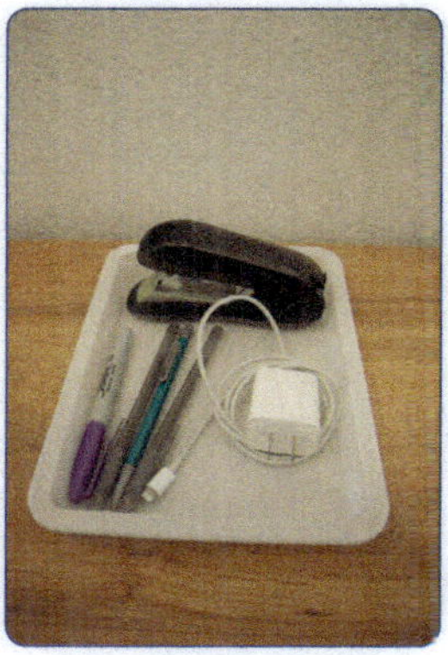

This one is a bit of a magic trick. Take five random items, like pens, a notebook, sticky notes, lip balm, and a phone charger. When you look at it, they scream clutter. But what happens when you put them into a small tray? Suddenly, they're not five random items, but one mini desk essentials kit. Gone is the idea of clutter. It's a psychological optical illusion, and it totally works. I absolutely live by this rule, as long as the tray is shallow and all items are visible. We're not looking for a new abyss.

These strategies can help you reduce the visual static that can build up and become overwhelming. Reducing the visual static isn't about creating a perfect home but about creating a moment of peace. You deserve a space that supports your brain, and not one that constantly argues with it.

CHAPTER TAKEAWAYS

01 The ADHD brain often struggles with object permanence, so if something's hidden, it might as well not exist.

02 One designated area near your main entryway can prevent the daily searching game.

03 ADHD-friendly workspaces should be distraction-limited and movement-tolerant. Keep only what you need in sight and rotate your tools often to keep the novelty alive.

04 Visual static can lead to avoidance and overwhelm. Calm your space by using trays, color clustering, and visual zoning to make it easier for your brain to process what it sees.

05 ADHD friendly spaces aren't about hiding your life in sleek boxes. It's about shaping your space to support how your brain functions. Clarity over aesthetics. Systems over stuff.

CHAPTER 8

WHEN YOU SHARE YOUR SPACE

> People with ADHD often have a special feel for life, a way of seeing right into the heart of matters, while others have to reason their way methodically.
>
> DR. EDWARD M. HALLOWELL

My father always used to say, "When I'm on my own, I'm a perfect person. It's when I have to deal with others that things go sideways." He meant this as a joke, but there's a lot of truth in it. It's easier to be kind, gentle, loving, and organized when you're by yourself. It can even be easier to manage your home, your office, and your closet when you're the only one using each space. But when other people and their quirks and needs are added to the mix, it can be tricky to manage the ADHD mind. Organizing is one thing when you're the only human using the space and a whole other adventure when the space is shared with kids, partners, and roommates who leave their socks everywhere.

When you live with others, not only do you need to find a way of organizing that works for everyone involved, but you also need commitment from everyone to stick to the systems. If you've ever carefully labeled a bin only to have someone dump random batteries, hair ties, and a half-eaten granola bar into it, you know exactly what I'm talking about. I've worked with many ADHDers who've tried to build systems only to have them unravel the minute another person enters the room. Let me tell you:

> There's no IKEA hack strong enough to fix a system that was never agreed on in the first place.

This chapter is about building shared spaces that work—not by turning your family into tiny clones of you (even though that does sound like fun), but by learning how to negotiate space, communicate needs, and build visual systems that everyone can understand and follow, even if they don't have ADHD. We'll dive into low-conflict communication scripts, which will allow you to negotiate your needs calmly. We'll also talk about teaching kids and partners in ways that are both respectful and realistic. Spoiler: Sometimes, it's about giving up the dream of a perfectly curated entryway and instead agreeing that the shoes will live in a basket.

If you've ever felt like you're constantly cleaning up behind people who don't see the mess the same way you do, or if you've struggled to explain why certain things feel chaotic to your brain when they don't bother anyone else, this is the chapter for you. Let's work together to create a space where everyone can feel at ease and maybe even remember where the scissors live.

MANAGING SHARED EXPECTATIONS WITHOUT CONFLICT

Living with others means navigating a world of different tolerances for clutter, noise, and visual order. And when neurodiverse and neurotypical brains share a space, these differences can feel especially pronounced. What often occurs is a clash of clutter tolerances. One person might feel calm amidst a bit of creative chaos, while another can't relax unless every item is in its designated spot. For someone with ADHD, a few dishes left in the sink might be a non-issue as the house is "clean enough," whereas the neurotypical partner might see it as a sign of impending doom. These differing perceptions aren't about right or wrong—they're about how our brains process our environments.

Neurodivergent individuals often experience heightened sensitivity to sensory input, making some clutter more of a nuisance than others. For example, even if the house is spotless, a loud television and the sound of the chopping board in the kitchen might be too much to deal with. A neurotypical individual might not understand why this can feel like clutter since the house appears clean to them. On the flip side, ADHDers might not notice the pile of mail growing on the counter, while that same pile is driving their non-ADHD partner insane.

The solution lies in finding a functionality threshold you both can agree on. This involves open, non-judgmental conversations about what each person needs to feel comfortable and functional in shared spaces. To help with discussions like this, you might want to ask the following questions:

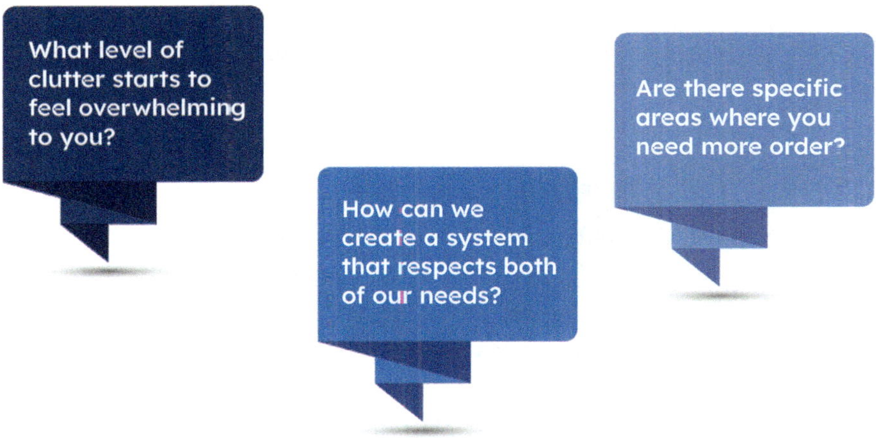

By identifying the threshold, you can co-create a living environment that feels supportive for everyone involved. However, please remember that the goal isn't perfection or agreeing on everything. The goal is to find functionality and mutual respect. It's okay if the shoes live in a basket and aren't perfectly lined up by the door. It's okay if the dumping zone isn't picture perfect. It's even okay to remind each other of the agreed-upon systems from time to time. And when things get messy (which they inevitably will), a little humor can go a long way. After all, sometimes laughter is the best way to diffuse tension over a misplaced remote or a forgotten load of laundry.

LOW CONFLICT COMMUNICATION SCRIPTS

Unfortunately, yelling at your spouse to "JUST PUT IT AWAY!" isn't an effective system. In fact, if we're being honest, it's not really a system at all. Advocating your needs in a shared space can feel like walking a tightrope over a volcano full of unspoken expectations and mismatched dishwashing standards. But here's the thing:

> Most of the time, conflict over mess isn't really about the mess at all. It's about miscommunication.

When you have different brains sharing one space, clarity, kindness, and collaboration become more important than ever. Advocating for your needs without sounding like you're nagging, accusing, or giving a TED talk can be tricky, which is why we need to all work on our communication skills.

So, where do we start? We need to build a communication toolkit that we can use, not to win arguments, but to create mutual understanding. That begins with language that's clear, non-accusatory, and focused on needs (and not blame). To build your toolkit, here are a few of my favorite ADHD-advocacy scripts. These are flexible, fill-in-the-blank-style prompts you can adapt depending on your space, your relationship, and your tone. The goal is to make it easier to speak up before things boil over into passive-aggressive cabinet slamming.

PROMPT 1: NEEDING A CLEAR SPACE

Instead of nagging the other person to clear the table or to stop dumping their things on the couch, let's communicate why it's important. Here's what you can say:

> **Hey, I know this might not look like a big deal, but I need this table clear because visual clutter makes it really hard for me to focus or even relax. Can we work together to figure out a way to keep just this one surface open at all times?**

The magic here lies in expressing what you need and why you need it. It's not just a quirk or you being difficult for no reason. You're owning your sensory threshold and giving context without framing it as a personal failure or someone else's fault.

PROMPT 2: REQUESTING CHANGE

If you need change, I suggest asking for it by explaining what you need and why it would be helpful to you. However, be sure to frame it as a question. You're not demanding that those around you change. Here's how you might say it:

By phrasing it as a question, your complaint is turned into a cooperative request. You're solving the problem together, and not throwing blame grenades. Be open to discussing possibilities with your roommate or partner to make sure you both are comfortable with the change.

PROMPT 3: WELCOMING TEAM WORK

You know what works for your brain and what doesn't. Sometimes, we can assume that those who live with us know this as well, but that's not always the case. In my early years of marriage, my husband often came up with "solutions" for me because he wanted to help. It took me years to learn how to express that, while I appreciated his help, his systems didn't always work for me and often made it worse. The solution? Asking him to help me solve problems as a team. Instead of shooting down his ideas or trying to do it all on my own, we began a collaborative approach. Here's how you might invite someone to help you:

> It helps me a lot when we keep chargers together so I always know where to find them. Could we find a bin for the chargers and make a label so that it can have a permanent home?

> I struggle with task initiation, but I'm way more likely to stay on track if we start together. Could we pick two days a week when we do the dishes together?

This works because you're not demanding perfection. Instead, you're inviting shared structure.

PROMPT 4: SHOWING SELF-AWARENESS

What bothers you might not bother others, and that's okay. One isn't necessarily right or wrong. It's just different. When you know something is bothering only you, it's okay to express and acknowledge that. It will show self-awareness and invite understanding. For example, instead of asking your partner to clear their side of the bathroom because it's a mess, explain why it's bothering you. You could try this:

> **Hi, I know that the bathroom clutter doesn't bug you like it does me, but it really overloads my brain, making it hard to feel completely clean and ready. Could we try using a tray or a drawer for the daily stuff instead of leaving it on the counter?**

In doing this, you're showing self-awareness and compassion while still making a clear task.

It's vital to consider your tone in all of this. How you say something is just as important as what you're saying. These scripts are designed to come from a place of curiosity and collaboration, not criticism. Here are a few quick tips to keep in mind:

- Use "I" statements, not "you" accusations. ("I get overwhelmed..." vs. "You always leave your stuff everywhere!")
- Frame it as a collaboration. ("Can we try..." or "Would it help if we...")
- Add some humor if it fits. Sometimes, a "Please help my goblin brain find the scissors" goes further than a formal plea.
- Get specific. Instead of "The house is a mess," try "Can we tackle the living room?"

The bottom line is that clear, kind communication will help you to advocate for your environment without shame or guilt. And when everyone understands the why behind your needs, they're more likely to support them.

BUILDING SHARED VISUAL SYSTEMS

Have you ever put the mail down on the table, only for it to disappear into the clutter-void two minutes later? One of the biggest challenges when it comes to shared spaces, especially with ADHD brains in the mix, is memory friction. Who was supposed to do what again? When is that permission slip due? Do socks go in the third or fourth drawer? This is where shared visual systems come in. Think of them as the external brains for your collective sanity. They aren't just cute DIY projects (even though they can be). They're functional, ADHD-friendly ways to reduce confusion, repetition, and oh-so-fun-passive-aggressive sighs in the hallway.

Visual systems work because they do two critical things:

OFFLOAD MEMORY	You no longer need to remember everything because you'll see what needs to go where.
CREATE CONSISTENCY	Everyone will know what to expect, and it completely removes the guesswork.

Table 6: Why visual systems work.

For ADHDers, this helps with object permanence and executive function. And for neurotypicals? It reduces the need for reminders and rediscovery loops. It's win-win for both. As productivity expert David Allen famously said, "Your brain is for having ideas, not holding them" (Allen, 2015). This is especially important when you're trying to get out the door with matching shoes. To create shared visual systems, here are a few real-life-tested ideas to turn your collective chaos into mutual calm.

THE FAMILY COMMAND CENTER

Some of the biggest fights in family homes are due to misplaced items. "Mom! He took my book!" or "Honey, did you take my keys again?" When everyone is to blame for everyone's items, it's chaos. How can we solve it? By creating a family command center. Set up a spot with a dry-erase calendar for everyone's appointments. If it's not on the family calendar, you can't blame anyone for not knowing about it. Say goodbye to last-minute bake sale reminders and birthday presents. Your command center also needs a corkboard for school flyers and other notes, as well as labeled baskets for each person. That way, it's no longer everyone's fault when someone loses their things. Everyone is in charge of their own belongings. Your command center can also benefit from a "today" board with who's doing what, so no one gets ambushed with surprise laundry.

COLOR-CODED CHORE MAGNETS

One of the other biggest reasons for conflict in homes is chores. Whether you have children, live with a roommate, or it's only you and your spouse, chores are often a point of conflict. The best way to solve this is by having a color-coded chore calendar where you divide weekly and daily chores fairly. Not only will you see what you and the other person are responsible for, but you can also keep track of what you still need to do. When it comes to children, this will help them to stop bickering over whose turn it is to do what. I also suggest having a fun reward system for when you complete your tasks. That way it's visible and satisfying.

FLOOR TAPE FOR BOUNDARIES

Boundaries are another reason for conflict. Some people can lose a sense of spatial awareness and impose without realizing it. Sometimes, you just need a break from your family and roommates, and the best way to ensure you always have space for yourself is by creating visible boundaries. One of my clients was nearing burnout with three children under the age of seven and felt the need for some alone space. “They're always on me. Even when I'm overwhelmed!” The solution? Literal floor tape. She made a line in front of her office door, which the children weren't allowed to cross. It was “Mom's space” and nothing else. But the tape also served a purpose for other things that needed boundaries. They used it to mark off a “toy corner” in the living room, as well as a “drop zone” where they could put anything they wanted for the day. This is a great way to teach spatial boundaries without constant nagging.

LABELED PAPERWORK BINS

The last major point of conflict is often about shared papers (the paper monster). To avoid this from happening, you can create a simple three-pile system in your drop zone or command center:

- Today: These are things that need to be dealt with now, like field trip slips and bills.
- In progress: These are papers that are waiting for a response or are in the middle of a task, such as taxes or renewal forms.
- To file: These are the things that need long-term homes, but not right this second.

To ensure that the labeled paperwork doesn't become another dumping ground, make sure it's labeled clearly and not located in a central part of the house.

These small changes can make a huge difference because instead of relying on one person to be the household memory hub, visual systems will distribute the responsibility. They also remove ambiguity, so there's no room for “I didn't know that was mine.” And perhaps best of all? You get fewer questions, more independence, and less explaining. A label can often speak louder than weeks of nagging.

TEACHING KIDS (AND SPOUSES)

No one wants to be a clutter cop for the rest of their lives, right? But it can be tricky to balance "I want my space to be ADHD friendly and organized" with "I don't want to keep nagging my family and asking the same thing a thousand times." Teaching your children, and possibly your spouse, how to manage the systems in place doesn't make you the fun police. It's all about flipping the script from "Why am I the only one who cares?" to "Let's be a team." This is where team mode comes in. In team mode, no one is the boos, the slacker, or the nag. Everyone has a role and one goal in mind: mutual support. Here are some examples of how you can accomplish team mode with children of all ages:

FOR TODDLERS: MAKE IT PLAYFUL

Toddlers won't care about your colorful chore chart. But you know what they will care about? The "clean-up" song while throwing blocks into a basket like they're scoring points in toddler basketball. To activate team mode with your toddler, make it fun and present it at a level they understand. Try basket pickups with a timer or a silly voice challenge. For example, "Can you beat the robot and pick up the most blocks?" You can also try giving them their own job, like putting all the pillows back or wiping the coffee table with a sock on their hand. Don't worry about perfection for now. We're building muscle memory and positive vibes, not Martha Stewart proteges.

FOR SCHOOL-AGE KIDS: SHOW, LABEL, REPEAT

These kiddos are at prime checklist age. And guess what? Most kids love visual cues just as much as ADHD adults do. To activate team mode with your school-age children, try using visual chore charts with bright colors and pictures, or create a checklist for before school and bedtime. It's important to hang the checklist somewhere they can look at it at eye level. Another idea is to create a one basket per child rule for stuff that belongs to them. What they leave in the basket in the living room or foyer is totally up to them as long as they take responsibility for it. Make it consistent, but don't be rigid about it. If you want to get maximum effort from them, invite them to help design the system. The more involved they are, the more they'll stick to the system.

FOR TEENS: AUTONOMY AND ACCOUNTABILITY

Teens need freedom. But as much as they might think they can handle life on their own, they also need a gentle container for that freedom. That's where bin-boundaries can come into play. You can try incorporating a bin system where they are responsible for a few bins around the house, as well as their own. Once a week, the bins need to be reset, and that can be their responsibility. Other tips you can use to activate team mode with your teen are by using tech-friendly reminders like a Google calendar or Alexa. You can also allow them to choose their reset rhythm. When do they want to clear the bins and reset for the week? This will keep things from morphing into the "Did you clean your room?" broken record and help build executive function over time.

FOR SPOUSES AND HOUSEMATES: DIVIDE BY ENERGY

We all have different rhythms. Some of us love organizing spices alphabetically (not me), while others can declutter a whole closet in a hyperfocus sprint Instead of equal division, aim for energy-matched division. For example, you can tell your partner, "You do the loud, fast stuff like vacuuming, and I'll do the calm repetitive stuff like folding laundry while I have my headphones on." You can also incorporate the method of body doubling. Body doubling is when you each have your own tasks, but you do them in the same room. This helps the

ADHD mind feel less lonely, and you are less likely to end up doom-scrolling instead. Above all, it's vital to have scheduled, shared resets. A quick 10-minute blitz with music and a clear goal is sometimes all you need to quickly make the house feel more livable again.

One of my clients, David, and his family have incorporated what they call the Sunday Night Crew. They all work together, choose a zone (yes, even the six-year-old), set a timer, and blast their favorite music (they take turns). It's not perfect, but they all work together, and it's much better than David yelling at the children to clean up the laundry or unpack the dishwasher.

When you shift your home from "This is my burden" to "This is our space," something beautiful happens. You stop feeling like the house manager and start feeling like a coach. One who sometimes forgets where the clipboard is, but the coach nonetheless. Creating systems together builds shared buy-in, reduces resentment, and honestly, helps the whole household breathe a little easier.

CHAPTER TAKEAWAYS

01 Team mode beats control mode. Instead of trying to manage everything on your own, create systems that involve everyone. It's about collaboration and not micromanagement.

02 Communication doesn't have to be confrontational. Saying what you need doesn't have to sound like a complaint. Using low-conflict scripts can help you to advocate for your needs in a way that invites cooperation.

03 Shared visual systems can save sanity and reduce memory strain.

04 Anyone at any age can contribute, even if it's only putting the remote in the right place.

05 Divide tasks by energy and not fairness. Instead of always aiming for a 50/50 core split, try assigning tasks based on energy, strength, and preference.

PART

04

STICKING TO IT

> For reasons we don't quite understand, soon after you command yourself to pay attention, you forget that you commanded yourself to pay attention.
>
> DR. EDWARD M. HALLOWELL

CHAPTER 9

HABIT STACKING THAT DOESN'T SUCK

> ADHD is not a disease; it's a different way of thinking and processing information.
>
> UNKNOWN

This might ruffle some feathers, but oh well. I'll forget that I said it in a minute: Most advice books about building habits are written by people who do not have an ADHD brain. You know, the books that say you need to "just" wake up at 5 a.m., meditate for 20 minutes, drink a green smoothie, and journal before sunrise to be happy. Meanwhile I'm over here trying to remember if I already brushed my teeth or if I just thought about brushing my teeth while scrolling on my phone. If you've ever tried to build a "better routine" and ended up in a shame spiral because it didn't stick, you're not alone, and you're not broken.

The ADHD brain isn't lazy or unwilling; it's just different, so it requires something different to build habits that last. That means fewer rules, more visuals, more dopamine, and a lot more grace! This chapter is your ADHD-friendly guide to habit stacking that doesn't suck. We'll talk about how to attach a new habit to something you're already doing (like a Post-it on your coffee mug), how to make habits visual and rewarding (hello, dopamine hit!), and why chasing motivation doesn't work, but chasing fun absolutely can.

ATTACHING NEW HABITS TO OLD ONES

You know that thing where you get up to grab a pair of socks and somehow end up cleaning the bathroom sink and re-potting a succulent instead? Yeah. That's part of the ADHD flavor, also known as context-based behavior. Our brains aren't great at holding long-term plans, but we are excellent at latching onto whatever's already happening in front of us. That's why the "When/Then" habit formula works so beautifully. The idea is simple: Instead of trying to create a habit out of thin air, you attach it to something you already do without thinking. You don't need motivation, you just need an anchor. Let me show you how this works in the wild:

- **When** I feed the dog, **then** I wipe down the counters. Feeding the dog happens every day without fail, because dogs are relentless, so now wiping the counters rides on that wave of consistency.
- **When** I make coffee, **then** I unload the dishwasher. Coffee is sacred. I'm not going to forget it. I'm pretty sure one day, when I'm on my deathbed, I'll whisper, "Double shot with almond milk, please." Pairing making coffee with a quick unload means I'm already standing in the kitchen, semi-conscious, with my hands free, waiting for the machine to do its thing.
- **When** I brush my teeth, **then** I spray the shower with cleaner. Two minutes of brushing is the perfect window for a quick spritz. No scrubbing, no drama, just a daily mist that keeps the grime from turning into a science experiment.
- **When** I walk in the door, **then** I hang my keys on the hook. This one saved me from endless "Where did I put my keys?" scavenger hunts. It also saved my family from watching me panic before every appointment.
- **When** I change my clothes, **then** I toss the dirty ones directly in the hamper. Because let's be honest, chairs weren't designed to be closets, but they often end up that way. However, by getting into the habit of

putting the dirty clothes in the hamper, I at least know the clothes on my chair are still wearable.

This is what I like to call the power of linkage. No motivation. No guilt. Just a good ol' contextual piggybacking. The trick is to start with ultra-simple, high-frequency habits. We're talking things you already do most days without needing a reminder. If you rarely floss but always check your phone when you sit down, then guess what? Your anchor isn't flossing, it's scrolling. So maybe: When I check my phone, then I stretch for 30 seconds. Here's your permission slip to start small. Stupidly small. Don't be overly ambitious with your pairings. Keep it as simple as "When I microwave leftovers, then I wipe one kitchen drawer handle." Don't try to do it all. Just take one thing at a time and teach your brain that it follows something else. That's it!

MAKE IT VISUAL

One of the best ways to ensure that everything you've learned so far doesn't disappear the moment you close this book is by making it as visual as possible. We've discussed object permanence in previous chapters, so this serves as a friendly reminder to make things as visual as possible. If you want to remember something consistently, you have to make it loud to your eyeballs. We've touched on some ways to do this, such as a command center, but here are a few other ideas on making reminders visible.

- **Dry erase boards in the bathroom:** Put a small dry erase board next to the mirror in your bathroom. Morning or evening routines? Right there in your face while you're brushing your teeth. Need a gentle reminder to take your meds? Write it there where you'll be able to see it first thing in the morning. Write it. Circle it. Put a star by it. Doodle a grumpy little cartoon yelling, "Moisturize your face, you beautiful lizard!" Use the board however you want, as long as it serves a purpose.

- **Icon-based checklists near workstations:** Words can blend into wallpaper after a while, but pictures still pop. Use simple visuals for things like "start timer," "reply to one email," or "check calendar." If your brain sees a tiny cartoon coffee cup and instantly thinks "get to work," you're golden. It doesn't have to make sense to everybody, just those using the checklists.
- **Sticker charts:** Yes, sticker charts work for grown-ups as well. Don't underestimate the dopamine rush of slapping a star on a chart. Want to track how often you take vitamins or stretch your back? Make it visible. Want to track your water intake? Create a fun chart and use stickers to mark off every cup of water you have. Make it fun! Allow yourself to feel inspired and motivated by things as simple as a "Well done!" sticker.

I have a personal, laminated habit tracker that's right next to my desk. Every night before I finish my work, I do a little check-in. Did I drink water? Feed my ADHD soul with some downtime? Did I stretch my crabby hips? That moment of visibility became a ritual. It's something I look forward to every single day. It's not another thing I forget, but a familiar cue that gently nudges me toward better choices.

Remember, the ADHD brain isn't lazy, and we're not forgetting things on purpose. We just have brains that file stuff in a different way. Visual cues help us externalize memory by turning invisible expectations into visible prompts. And no, this doesn't mean turning your home into a preschool classroom (unless that's your aesthetic, then go for it!). It means creating a home that reminds you of what you want to do, not just what you've been forgetting. Visuals keep us on track, nudges us forward, and let us off the hook from having to mentally juggle every single step of the day. It's not cheating; it's strategy.

CHASE THE DOPAMINE HIGH

Dopamine is the magical brain juice that fuels attention, motivation, and the giddy thrill of crossing things off a list. For ADHD brains, dopamine is in short supply, especially when a task feels boring, repetitive, or just ugh (Barkley, 2012). In other words, we're neurologically wired to seek stimulation that gives our brains the oomph to get going. If you've ever wondered why you can scroll TikTok for an hour but not send one email, it's because you've met your dopamine system. ADHD isn't always a lack of attention; it's a lack of interest-driven dopamine regulation. Translation? We don't chase boring things. The goal is to work with your brain instead of guilt-tripping it into oblivion, and to do so, we need to build a reward right into the habit itself. You can hack your habits to deliver micro-doses of dopamine. It's like tricking your brain, but in a nice way. Here's how:

STICKER CHARTS FOR COMPLETED ROUTINES

We just spoke about the power of stickers, and this is proof that it works. This is a hill I'm willing to die on: Sticker charts aren't just for preschoolers. That shiny gold star or sparkly unicorn sticker feels good! Every time you slap one down after doing your daily reset or remember to take your meds, your brain goes, "Ooh, we did something! Look at us go!" It acts as motivation because it gives you just enough dopamine to keep going and look for more (Littman, 2025).

TOKEN OR MARBLE JARS

This is a classic ADHD-friendly visual reward system. Every time you do the thing you want or need to do, like unpacking the dishwasher or drinking water, toss a token into a jar. Why does this work? Because you get to watch the jar fill up. With every token added to the jar, you'll feel motivated to add another and another and another, and before you know it, you've built a healthy habit. This is also a great way to see progress. Oftentimes, we are so hard on ourselves because we fail to do one thing. But with all the tokens present, you can remind yourself of all the things you didn't fail to do, and find motivation and encouragement in previous wins. You can also add some milestones to your jar. Quarter filled to the top? Time to reward yourself with your favorite Thai food for lunch! All the way to the top? Let's take the day off and do only fun things!

APP-BASED REWARDS

If you're more into digital tools, I suggest checking out apps like *Habitica* (which turns your life into a role-playing game) or *Forest* (where you grow a virtual tree by staying focused). These tools build gamification into tedious tasks and reward you instantly, without needing a real-life sticker drawer (but no judgment if you have one). By using these apps, you can also incorporate small rewards and mini celebrations. For example, if you've done a one-hour push of work, you get to doom scroll for 10 minutes. Or if you folded the laundry, enjoy a fancy coffee with foam and cinnamon sprinkles. That little bit of positive reinforcement rewires your brain to associate success with something good, which helps override the executive function fog that says "meh" to everything.

One of my clients, a brilliant but scatterbrained college student named Jake, used to avoid reading as if it were radioactive. So, we built a habit stack with a reward system: When he finished a 25-minute Pomodoro study session, he got one 5-minute YouTube video of his choice. Suddenly, he was flying through assignments and even added a second time session just to get to the next video. Gamification for the win! But why does this work?

Dopamine helps regulate focus, motivation, and emotional reward (Silva, 2024). So, if you feel bad for "bribing" yourself—don't. Feel empowered that you understand how your brain works and you're building habits that work with it, not against it. So, go ahead. Celebrate the little stuff! Make your wins loud, visible, and yes, even a little silly! Because repetition doesn't have to suck when you actually look forward to it!

CHAPTER TAKEAWAYS

01 Instead of relying on willpower, attach a new action to something you're doing by using the when/then method.

02 Visual cues are your best friend, so use tools like checklists and habit trackers to reduce the mental load and make routines more automatic.

03 Keep new habits small and easy to set yourself up for success. Small wins build momentum, leading you to larger and larger wins.

04 Dopamine makes habits stick, so use it to reward and motivate yourself.

05 Boring equals forget-able in the ADHD brain, so make it fun! Sing a reset song, track your streak, and reward yourself with coffee or a nap or whatever makes you excited and keeps you coming back for more.

CHAPTER 10

YOUR ENERGY IS THE SCHEDULE

> ADHD isn't about a lack of effort; it's about a different kind of energy.
>
> UNKNOWN

Let me tell you a hard truth I had to learn (and re-learn about 73 times): A schedule only works if your brain and body show up for it. I used to print out perfect color-coded planners. You know, the ones with hour-by-hour blocks where 9 a.m. is "respond to emails," and 10 a.m. is "deep focus work." But what actually happened at 9 a.m.? Well, every day was different. Some mornings, I was ready for a deep focus, while other mornings, I was still under the covers, wondering why cereal tastes better after midnight and how planes stay in the air (I'm still unsure).

> The thing is, ADHD isn't a time management problem; it's an energy management problem.

You might not know what day it is, but you definitely know when your brain is firing on all cylinders or when it's doing that buffering wheel thing again. You can have the perfect schedule on paper, but if your energy isn't there, it won't help you. In fact, it might just make you feel even worse. That's why, in this chapter, we're tossing the rigid, soul-crushing productivity templates and replacing them with something more ADHD-friendly: weekly energy mapping. That means learning when you have focus, motivation, or even the will to put on pants and building your to-dos around that reality.

We'll also talk about what to do when everything goes sideways because (spoiler alert) something will. I'll walk you through how to create a gentle, no-shame reset for bad days that helps you get back on track without judgment, tears, and burning it all down. This chapter is for anyone who's ever stared at their calendar and thought, "Absolutely not." Let's make a rhythm that fits your brain and honors the fact that your energy isn't a machine. It's a wave, and we need to learn how to ride it.

WEEKLY ENERGY MAPPING

Alright, my fellow ADHDer, it's time to grab a highlighter, some sticky notes, or a scrap of junk mail from under your couch. We're about to do something wild: Stop scheduling our lives like a boring robot and start building them around our actual human energy. Because here's the ADHD truth:

> Time-blocking works great in theory, but energy is what decides whether we actually unload the dishwasher or just open it, stare at the clean plates, and close it again like it's a haunted tomb.

Traditional planners assume we can do the same task at the same time and at the same pace every day, which we absolutely cannot. Some mornings, I can work for four hours straight, while other mornings, four minutes is a struggle. Our brains operate more like jazz music: improvisational, slightly chaotic, but brilliant when in rhythm. Instead of asking, *When should I do this?* try asking yourself, *When does this match my energy?* This is the core idea behind energy-based planning: to organize your home care tasks based on how much juice you realistically have in the tank, and not what the clock says. Here's what that might look like in real life. First, you need to identify how much energy certain tasks require of you:

LOW-ENERGY MOMENTS (a.k.a. "Do not disturb unless on fire" mode) might include	• Wipe counters. • Toss trash in a bin • Sort one drawer while sitting down. • Move laundry from washer to dryer (no folding required).
MEDIUM-ENERGY MOMENTS (a.k.a. "Functional but snack-dependent" mode) will look something like:	• Do a 10-minute room reset. • Fold and put one load of laundry away. • Clear out the fridge. • Water the plants before they start screaming
HIGH-ENERGY MOMENTS (a.k.a. "In the zone, babe" mode) can include:	• Reorganize the pantry. • Deep clean the bathroom. • Tackle the junk drawer. • Declutter the top of the dresser that's become a shrine to random receipts.

Table 7: Energy mapping and task examples.

But how do we know when to do what if we can't schedule it ahead of time? You can start by following these three simple steps:

STEP 1: TRACK YOUR RHYTHMS

Start by noticing your energy patterns throughout the week. Not what you wish they were, but what they actually are. For a few days, jot down when you feel:

- focused and alert
- zoning out while staring at a spoon
- cranky, crashy, or nap-prone
- able to get into flow
- drained just from thinking about moving

You can become aware of these moments by asking yourself some basic questions, such as:

- *When do I naturally get things done?*
- *When do I hit a wall?*
- *What time of day do I want to hide from everything?*
- *What drains me fast, even if it seems small?*

For me, Monday mornings are a big nope. I don't wake up motivated and energized after the weekend, no matter how well I rested. I don't see it as "fresh new week to make things happen." I dread it. So, that's when I light a candle and do easy jobs. I tackle some basic admin to make the following day easier and respect my lack of motivation. But on Wednesdays? I'm alive! I can focus for hours, finally motivated by a "new week." By noticing your natural flow, you can start to build a mental (or visual) map of your weekly energy zones. You can draw them out, color-code it, or use a digital tool.

STEP 2: MATCH THE TASK TO THE ENERGY

Now that you know your high, medium, and low patterns, start pairing tasks to them. This helps reduce shame spirals from "I should've done more," and replaces them with "That was a low-energy hour. I did what low-energy me could do." You'll begin to see that you're not lazy or inconsistent; you're cycling energy just like everyone else. You just need to plan accordingly.

STEP 3: LET IT FLEX

The goal isn't to lock tasks into a rigid schedule, because even with patterns in mind, our energy might not always behave the same way. Some Mondays I feel great, and some Wednesdays are worse than Mondays! That's why we need to keep this plan fluid, like your brain. It's permission to pivot! If you thought it was a "reorganize the spice rack" day, but your soul says no? Pivot! Wipe the stove and leave the rest for tomorrow. It's not failure, it's strategy.

A RESET FOR BAD DAYS

Some days are just... toast. You wake up and without warning, your brain is like, "Yeah, no. We're not doing that today." Your body's moving through Jell-O, and everything feels too much, including the idea of deciding what to do. Executive function has left the building without leaving a forwarding address. What now? Do we collapse under a weighted blanket until further notice? If you can, that would be great. But I'm not sure if your manager will take kindly to it (or your toddler). Instead, let's activate the bad day backup plan, or as I like to call it, the 3D method. This system has helped me on numerous occasions, and I use it whenever I'm feeling overwhelmed, under-caffeinated, or just vibing at sea-level energy. It helps me shift out of shame and into preservation mode, which is still a win!

Let's break it down. When your brain says, "Nope," this method says, "Okay, let's adjust." It doesn't try to force your brain to "get over itself" or "do it anyway." We know that tough love often only makes it worse the next day, so let's embrace kindness as we look at the three Ds.

STEP 1: DROP

When you feel stuck in a bad day, the first thing you need to ask yourself is *What can I drop today?* In other words, what tasks don't need your attention today? I promise you, the world won't implode if you don't open the mail or fold the laundry. What can you drop without truly hurting anything? Can you drop your child's recital without hurting them? No, so keep it on the schedule. But can you drop unpacking the dishwasher and sweeping the floor? Yes. Can you drop showing up to work on time? No. But can you drop that check-in with your colleague that's not urgent? Yes. Choosing things that can weigh you down and actively removing them from your schedule can do wonders in releasing the pressure.

STEP 2: DELEGATE

You don't have to do everything alone. Even if your brain tells you otherwise, you can ask others for help. ADHD often whispers, "No one else will do it right," but let's clap back with, "Done is better than perfect." So, ask yourself: *What's one thing someone else can do for me?* Instead of cooking dinner, ask your partner to take charge, even if it's takeout. Instead of using all your energy to bring in the trash bins, text your teen to ask for help. Even if you just delegate to your future self, it still counts. You're giving yourself a break now and removing things from your plate.

STEP 3: DEFER

Some tasks feel urgent, but they're not. The trick is to consciously move them, rather than letting them swirl around in your head like mental fruit flies. Ask yourself: *What can I defer with intention, and when will I pick it up again?* Deep-cleaning the sink? That can wait until Saturday. Sorting school papers? Tomorrow morning after coffee. Write it down and physically remove the deferred tasks from your daily planner. It will help your brain to relax and remove the weight of the world it's feeling.

You don't need to "win" every day. You just need to float through some of them. That's where the bare minimum checklist can be helpful. What is it? It's a simple checklist with three to five micro-actions on it that create a sense of safety, calm, and cleanliness without demanding perfection. By using the 3D method, you can remove anything from your day that isn't on your bare minimum checklist. Here's my bare minimum checklist for low-functioning days:

- Rinse dishes in the sink.
- Take out any trash that smells.
- Clear a walkway through the main space.
- Eat something protein-ish.
- Change out of pajamas, or into fresh ones.

Remember, on hard days, the goal isn't productivity; it's preservation. You're keeping the lights on and the vibes survivable. That's enough. That's huge, actually. I once spent a whole day moving laundry from the washer to the dryer and then just staring at it. That was my Everest. But you know what? I still rinsed a few dishes, fed myself some popcorn, and texted my friend that I was in slug mode. That's a win for me. When we acknowledge our limits and respond with kindness instead of shame, we're practicing a deeper kind of success. One rooted in respect for our brains, our bodies, and our very real needs.

If you're on a "bad brain day," don't push harder. Pull back. Drop. Delegate. Defer. And do the bare minimum with maximum grace.

CHAPTER TAKEAWAYS

01 ADHD brains don't run on strict clocks; we run on energy levels. Organizing tasks by low, medium, and high energy windows will help you work with your brain and not against it.

---

02 Map your energy, not just your week. Not all hours are created equal, so track your rhythm and use the info to schedule tasks that match your available energy.

---

03 The 3D method will help you to save the day when your brain feels fried. Let go of anything that's not essential and hand off what you can.

---

04 Even on your worst days, it's good to do something. A bare minimum checklist can help you to keep the wheels on without pushing yourself over the edge.

---

05 Compassion is more powerful than a planner, so be kind to yourself. Your value doesn't decrease with your energy levels. You're allowed to rest, reset, and be amazing.

PART

05

SEVEN DAYS TO SEE YOUR SPACE DIFFERENTLY

"

Your ADHD mind isn't a mistake—it's a masterpiece of possibility.

DR. DALE ARCHER

CHAPTER 11

THE FUNCTIONAL FREEDOM SPRINT

> Your biggest challenges have become your greatest strengths. That's not just survival—that's triumph.
>
> SAMANTHA CRAFT

It's time to buckle up. We're about to do something wild and spicy. Welcome to the Functional Freedom Sprint, a seven-day, no-perfection-allowed challenge designed specifically for our gloriously distracted, occasionally motivated, wonderfully wired ADHD brains. This is not about organizing your entire house from floor to ceiling like a Pinterest robot. This is about momentum and tiny, visible wins. It's about reclaiming function and freedom without needing a three-week planning session and 27 bins from The Container Store. Each day, you'll tackle one very doable thing that makes your space more functional. But don't worry, every task will come with:

- a low-energy version, because I know we sometimes run on fumes
- a dopamine boost idea, because we need to have fun and motivate ourselves
- a clear, visible win, so you can feel the progress

This isn't about creating the perfect, clean home. It's about doing something intentional that will make tomorrow feel a little lighter and better. You've got this! Focus on one day at a time. Ready? Let's sprint toward a little more sanity and a lot more function.

DAY 1: CLEAN ONE SURFACE

Welcome to Day 1 of your Functional Freedom Sprint, a.k.a. "Seven Days to Get Out of Clutter Jail." Today's mission is simple, visible, and satisfying: Pick one flat surface and give it a glow up. Why a surface? Because nothing screams "fresh start" like a countertop that isn't hosting an accidental science experiment. Since our brains crave visible order, one clean space can become your calm anchor. It serves as proof of progress! I've found that after I clean one surface, I am more likely to return to that area just to admire my own hard work. It inspires me to keep going and motivates me to keep it clean (at least for a few days).

So, what are we targeting? Pick a high-traffic or high-visibility flat surface. Don't choose that one corner in the house that no one goes to. Think kitchen counter, desk, nightstand, or coffee table.

YOUR STEPS

1. **Clean everything off:** It's time to clean everything off the surface. Like *everything*! Move it all to one side or use a bin or a basket for the time being. No judgment for the crumbs, loose hair ties, or ten pens you forgot existed. Just a clear surface.
2. **Group like with like:** Next, toss the trash and sort the rest. Put all the "officey" things together, all the "bedtime" items, etc. This gives you an instant sense of order, and it makes it easier to relocate the stray cheese stick wrapper.

3. **Wipe down the surface:** Once you've grouped everything and removed it from the surface, give the surface a quick clean. A simple swipe with a baby wipe or microfiber cloth will do the trick. Bonus point if you use soap or a scent you like. This is your fresh start moment. Enjoy it!
4. **Put back only what belongs:** Begin to put things back onto the surface, but only the things that really belong there. Ask yourself, "Do I use this here?" If not, it should go elsewhere. Keep the surface minimal, but functional.
5. **Relocate or toss the rest:** Don't stress about "finishing" the cleanup today. Give the items that don't belong on the surface you cleaned a temporary home, even if it's a bin or a box. You can revisit these items later if you have the energy.

LOW-ENERGY VERSION

If the above steps seem impossible and you've lost all your energy to be productive, that's okay. Don't bully yourself into doing something when your body and mind didn't show up to the party. Instead, take it easy and clear and wipe just one corner of the surface. Even if it's just one foot square, it counts. Why is it important to do something even when you don't feel like it? Because it will help alleviate subconscious guilt, reduce visual noise, and generally improve your life. You might not feel it in the moment, but when you wake up tomorrow morning and see that one clean corner, it will do wonders for your mind and mood.

DOPAMINE BOOST

If you need a little extra dopamine today, take a moment to gamify the cleaning. Set a two-song playlist timer and race the music to finish cleaning your surface. You can also light a nice-smelling candle while you work, making it a special moment. Additionally, take a before-and-after photo as motivation and show it to a friend who supports your journey!

WHY IT WORKS

The ADHD brain needs quick feedback loops and visible success to fuel momentum (Barkley, 2011). A clear surface will provide immediate sensory relief and give your brain a chance to anchor focus and confidence, especially if you pass by it regularly throughout the day. But remember, the goal isn't perfection, it's progress. And guess what? You've already started!

DAY 2: CREATE ONE DROP ZONE

Today is Day 2 of your Functional Freedom Sprint, also known as "Let's Not Lose Our Wallet (Again)." Today's goal is simple, powerful, and life-changing: We're creating your drop zone. What is a drop zone again? It's a small, designated spot near your front door (or wherever you usually fling things when you walk in) where your daily chaos can land with purpose. Your mission is simple: Pick a small area near your entry. Choose the entryway you use the most, whether it's the front door, side door, garage entry, teleportation portal, etc. This is where the daily avalanche of keys, sunglasses, mail, receipts, dog leashes, and headphones will go, without disappearing into the void.

YOUR STEPS

1. **Pick a landing spot:** The first thing your drop zone needs is a space. Choose a table, shelf, wall hook, or crate flipped sideways to serve as your drop zone area. Use whatever works with your space and doesn't annoy future you.
2. **Add a few containers:** Use some containers to help organize the space. For example, add hooks for keys, a small bowl or tray for your pocket stuff, and a mail tray or folder for incoming papers. You can also add a label that says "Drop Zone" if you want to be official.

3. **Test run it immediately:** Walk outside, come back in, and pretend you're arriving home. Did you have a place to drop all your gremlins? If yes, great! The system works. If not, tweak it until you do.

LOW-ENERGY VERSION

If you're feeling meh and you don't have the energy to create a whole drop zone, do the 30-second version. Hang one hook, put a bowl on the table, and walk away. That's it. Even that one hook and bowl will make future you weep with gratitude the next time you don't have to spend 10 minutes looking for your keys.

DOPAMINE BOOST

If you want to turn your drop zone into a dopamine boost, make it cute or visually appealing. Use a bowl or basket that makes you happy to look at it. It can be something from your grocery store, a thrift shop, or even a random container you forgot you owned. One of my clients is very into Star Wars, so he themed his drop zone accordingly. He made his basket look like a droid, so every time he gets home, he is excited to "feed" his droid all the junk in his pockets. Remember, this is your zone, so make it personal and functional for you. While it doesn't have to be Pinterest-worthy, it also doesn't have to be boring or ugly.

WHY IT WORKS

ADHD brains need clear external systems to reduce cognitive overload. A drop zone acts as a visual routine anchor, helping you automate decision-making around the daily dump zone. Plus, it cuts down on repetitive quests for keys and wallets. As long as the drop zone catches your stuff before the floor does, it's effective.

DAY 3: ORGANIZE ONE DRAWER

Okay, my fellow ADHDer, today is Day 3 of the Functional Freedom Sprint, and today we're tackling a tiny pocket of chaos: the drawer. Not every drawer. Not all drawers. Just one drawer—the one that gives you a mini eye twitch every time you open it. This could be the junk drawer in your kitchen (yes, the one with a single AA battery and 17 unused chopsticks), your desk drawer (hello, dried-out pens and expired gum), or the bathroom drawer where your floss goes to die. It's time to reclaim this tiny space and turn it from a mystery grab bag into a functional little friend.

YOUR STEPS

1. **Pick the drawer:** If your gut says, "No! Not that one!" then congratulations: That's the one you need to tackle. Trust the groan. If you tackle the one that scares you the most, it will also provide you with the most mental relief and satisfaction.
2. **Empty it:** Once you've picked your drawer, empty it completely. Remove every single item. Dump it on a towel or a tray so things don't roll away, but get it all out. And who knows? Perhaps you'll find a forgotten $5 or your long-lost nail clippers, boosting dopamine already!
3. **Group by function:** Group everything together so you know what's actually in there and what the drawer is used for most. Put pens with pens, cords with cords, and so on.
4. **Toss or rehome:** If you've found seven dead pens, it's time to toss them. Those manuals for appliances you don't own anymore? Bye! Use a trash bag like it's a boss battle and get rid of anything you can no longer use or need.

5. **Return only the essentials:** It's crucial to return only the essentials to the drawer. However, before you chuck everything back into the drawer, try using some dividers. Use little tins or food containers that no longer have lids and separate the categories. The ADHD brain will love the visual structure.

LOW-ENERGY VERSION

If you're low on vibes and energy, don't worry. All you have to do is open the drawer and remove five items that don't belong there. Challenge yourself to throw away one of the five and rehome the other four. Close the drawer and that's it. Even this mini move reduces your brain's clutter drag and frustration.

DOPAMINE BOOST

If you need a little pick-me-up during the cleaning, play a motivational song like "Eye of the Tiger." Additionally, if someone else is home, ask them to body double with you. This will help you to stay on track and to enjoy the process more.

WHY IT WORKS

Drawers are small, fast wins with big impact. Organizing one gives a sense of completion and order, which ADHDers thrive on when it's visible and tactile. Plus, removing friction from every task, like not having to dig for scissors or your meds, will boost your overall executive function, one drawer at a time.

DAY 4: RESET ONE FRICTION POINT

Because you don't want to fight the snack drawer every morning, welcome to Day 4 of the Functional Freedom Sprint. This day can also be called the day we have a calm, strategic stare-down with that one spot. You know the one. The place in your home that constantly whispers, "I dare you to put something here without it turning into chaos." Today is about tackling that friction point. It's not the same as the drop zone, though. It might not be the place where you dump your stuff as soon as you get home, but rather the space that tends to clutter up the fastest when you're home. This might be something like a vanity table or the coffee table in the living room.

A friction point can be identified as the spot that causes dread, mini rage, and repetitive clutter. It's that spot that no matter how often you clean it, it seems to come back worse within minutes. Common culprits include kitchen counters, snack cabinets, or that chair that catches all the clothes (the Throne of Clothes). So, let's reset it for success.

YOUR STEPS

1. **Identify the spot:** What area makes you sigh, roll your eyes, or just avoid it altogether? What spot is like a magnet for everyone and everything? That's the area we are working with today. It is possible to have more than one friction point, but we're only tackling one today. Choose the one you dread the most or the one that is most central to everyone in the house.
2. **Reset to neutral:** Set 10 minutes on the clock and begin to clear the friction spot. Ask yourself, *What's the minimum version of clean that still feels good to me?*" Remember, the friction point doesn't have to be completely empty. It should just not add more weight and mental clutter. Keep only the essentials to create a neutral place.
3. **Add a micro habit:** Next, add a micro habit to help keep this friction point neutral for longer. For example, add the micro habit of tossing the junk mail in the bin instead of on the coffee table. Or, add a two-minute "Everyone takes their stuff out of the living room" ritual before dinner each night. The goal is to create a micro habit that will allow you to reset the friction zone within a few minutes.

LOW-ENERGY VERSION

If you're overwhelmed or tired, you don't have to clean up the entire friction zone. Pick three things that don't belong and stop there. Step back. Take a breath. And celebrate the progress.

DOPAMINE BOOST

Need a little dopamine boost while cleaning the friction zone? Let's gamify it by creating mini challenges within the cleaning. Can you spot three things you left in the friction zone last night? What type of items are filling up the friction zone the most? Look for patterns and pretend to be a detective working a case while cleaning the fiction zone.

WHY IT WORKS

Resetting friction points gives visible wins in the exact spots where your energy usually drains. It's a strategic fix, not a cosmetic one. When you define "neutral" and make it easy to return to that state, you reduce cognitive drag and increase daily flow.

DAY 5: SPEED CLEAN 10 MINUTES

Did you know you can do literally anything... for 10 minutes? That's the theme of Day 5 of the Functional Freedom Sprint. This day can also be referred to as the ADHD-friendly version of a cleaning montage. Today's challenge is to harness the magic of short bursts, channel your inner domestic ninja, and clean as if a surprise guest just texted: "We're five minutes away." The goal isn't perfection or deep cleaning underneath the fridge (Wait, we're supposed to do that sometimes?). The goal is simply to make the house feel clean enough and tidy enough so you can relax and feel at home.

YOUR STEPS

Today's steps will be a little different because they come with a checklist. Instead of following three steps, you'll have one overarching step: See how many things you can tick off the checklist within 10 minutes. Start by putting a timer on and choose to blast some music (if you want to). Then, hit the zones where the clutter tends to collect like it's being paid. Here's your 10-minute speed clean checklist to follow.

- ☐ Toss visible trash.
- ☐ Gather dirty dishes and load them.
- ☐ Clear one surface.
- ☐ Pick up laundry on the floor or chair.
- ☐ Straighten pillows and blankets.
- ☐ Put shoes in their place.
- ☐ Wipe down a bathroom sink.
- ☐ Dump expired food from the fridge.
- ☐ Corral stray items into a bin or basket.
- ☐ Light a candle or spray a scent to signal it's done.

Ten items in ten minutes and you're done for the day. Easy enough, right? It might sound impossible, but test yourself and see how far you can get. You also don't have to follow the checklist in a linear fashion. If you want to start in the bathroom, be my guest. Whatever gets you going for ten minutes.

LOW-ENERGY VERSION

If you're low on energy, modify the checklist by limiting it to three things. Instead of time pressure, pick three items from the list that you need to complete before the end of the day. If you want to do one and rest for 30 minutes before doing the second, you're more than welcome to do so. Remove the time pressure and allow yourself to move at the pace of a snail.

DOPAMINE BOOST

To boost dopamine with the 10-minute clean, reward yourself immediately after the push. Have a dance party in your clean home, enjoy a cup of coffee, or scroll through some memes—you've earned it! You can also use a fun app that turns tasks into achievements. This will boost your dopamine just enough to keep going and complete the checklist. Remember, you're not being lazy. You just need a little bit of novelty and structure to get the wheels turning.

WHY IT WORKS

Speed cleaning works because it produces visible progress. Even one clean space can shift your mood and momentum entirely. Since the ADHD struggles with time blindness and initiation, these short burst with immediate feedback is a magical combination.

DAY 6: CREATE A RITUAL

Consistency doesn't have to be boring. So far, you've shown up every day. You've cleaned surfaces, battled rogue socks, and set timers like a boss. But now it's time to turn progress into a ritual. What is a ritual? It's something small, repeatable, and almost sacred (but you know, ADHD-friendly sacred). Why is a ritual important on Day 6 of your Functional Freedom Sprint? Because they're like a little autopilot function for your mind. They create structure without stress, and that's exactly what our ADHD brains crave but rarely find in the wild. When something becomes a ritual, it shifts from "Ugh, I have to" to "Oh, this is just what I do."

YOUR STEPS

For today, the steps might look different depending on what ritual you choose to implement. Start by picking one space you think can benefit from a ritual. It might be your bedroom, the kitchen counter, or your home office desk. Once you've chosen the area, you can begin to brainstorm possible rituals that the area could benefit from. The goal is to make the ritual as effortless and natural as possible. It also needs to be personal, so I won't be able to guide you much. However, I can provide some simple examples that could trigger an idea that's personal to you.

1. **Morning sweep:** After you brush your teeth in the morning, do a quick reset in your bedroom. Make your bed, fluff the pillows, and take yesterday's coffee mug back to the sink. This will go well with brushing teeth, as it will set your brain into "It's time to be ready for a new day" mode.
2. **Evening reset:** After you plug in your phone, wipe down one surface and toss couch blankets into a cozy pile, ready for the next morning.
3. **Sunday prep:** Reset your drop zone for the week, making sure everything you need is in the right place and everything that doesn't belong there is removed.

It's vital not to see these as chores, but as acts of peacekeeping. Rituals are calm and peaceful, not filled with manic energy that requires management. You're just building a new life, one habit-link at a time.

LOW-ENERGY VERSION

The point of a ritual is repetition, right? The goal of a low-energy version is not to create a ritual that always runs on low energy (because our energy levels won't always be low), but rather to have a toned-down version of our ritual for those days when energy is running low. So, when creating your ritual, determine a bare minimum for it to work. In other words, if your ritual is to do a quick reset in your bedroom every morning after brushing your teeth, the bare minimum might be as simple as making your bed. You don't have to sweep, clear a surface, or fluff the pillow. Just make the bed. Then, when your energy returns tomorrow, you can go back to the normal level of activity.

DOPAMINE BOOST

If you need a little motivation and a dopamine boost to create your ritual, use a visual tracker with stickers to help you keep track and remind you of the habit you're building. You can also choose to name your ritual something fun. Instead of "clean the counter," call it "Operation Sparkly Zone." Is it silly? You bet. But guess what makes your brain happy? Silliness and fun!

WHY IT WORKS

Rituals work because they anchor our attention. They reduce cognitive overwhelm and make it easier to stay consistent because they're tied to existing actions, like brushing teeth or making coffee. In ADHD land, consistency happens when friction is low and payoff is high. Remember, this is about creating small, repeatable rituals that support your sanity. Don't overcomplicate it.

DAY 7: CELEBRATE AND REFLECT

You've made it to the final day of the Functional Freedom Sprint! That's seven days of decluttering, dopamine-boosting, and executive functioning-wrangling. In ADHD years, that's basically a decade of progress. I'm so proud of you, and you should be proud of yourself, too! But before we rush off to the next shiny idea, let's take this last day to reflect. Why? Because reflection leads to reinforcement. And reinforcement means our ADHD brains will remember that what we've done worked. Without taking a beat to acknowledge your wins, your brain may just file this under "random chaos" and move on. So, let's reflect.

YOUR STEPS

Today's steps will be divided into two major parts. First, take a breath and ask yourself some questions. These prompts aren't just busywork. They will help your brain to store the success file where it can find it next time.

- What felt easiest this week? (You might be surprised).
- What was the hardest part? (It's okay to acknowledge that you struggled with something.)
- What surprised you the most?
- How do you feel in your space right now?
- Which day's task are you most proud of?

You can jot your answers in a journal, voice note, text it to your best friend, or shout it into the void while holding a mug of tea like a life coach. Just acknowledge your wins and your progress because they count.

The next step is to reward yourself. Yes, really. The ADHD brain responds beautifully to external motivation and celebration. So, choose something that makes you feel seen and successful. Here are some fun ideas:

- Take a photo of your favorite space and post it, or admire it secretly.
- Buy a small treat you've been eyeing and don't feel any guilt.
- Create a little "before and after" collage and do a happy dance!
- Share your win with someone who gets it (or your pet).

LOW-ENERGY VERSION

If you're not feeling like the whole reflection journaling thing today, that's okay. Do this instead:

- Name one thing that feels better in your home right now.
- Give yourself one kind word or a high-five.
- Put a sticker or draw a smiling face on your hand.

WHY IT WORKS

Reflection runs fleeting success into repeatable motivation. When you celebrate, you're reinforcing the behavior loop that makes future organization more likely. Plus, you deserve joy for your effort, not just function. Is the goal spotless drawers and clean freezers? No. The goal is to have more tools in your arsenal to manage your environment in a way that helps you see that you're not broken.

Hey, I know sprints can feel like a lot sometimes. But if all you did this week was try a few of these things, or even think about trying them, you're already rewiring how you relate to your space. That's not nothing. It's the start of something. Now, take a breath. Have a cookie. And when you're ready, I'll meet you in the next chapter.

CHAPTER TAKEAWAYS

01 Small wins are powerful. You don't need to overhaul your entire house. Just cleaning one surface or organizing one drawer can create a visible and emotional shift. You deserve to feel that shift.

02 Structure doesn't mean rigidity. This seven-day sprint wasn't about perfection, but about giving you a roadmap that flexes with your energy. Low-barrier options and dopamine boosts? Totally legal and advised.

03 Your space affects your brain. Visual clutter equals mental clutter. But now you've got tools to interrupt the chaos and reclaim calm. Cleaning one hotspot is basically like therapy, but cheaper.

04 You're building more than habits. You are building momentum! Repetition with reward wires your brain for follow-through. The more you celebrate, the more your brain says, "Hey, let's do that again."

05 Reflection seals the deal. Acknowledging what worked helps make it stick. You're not just surviving your home, you're shaping it to serve you.

PART

06

RELAPSE-PROOF YOUR PROGRESS

> Sometimes, I've got too many thoughts at once. It's like there's a four-way intersection in my brain where everyone's trying to go at the same time.
>
> A. J. FINN

CHAPTER 12

WHEN IT ALL FALLS APART AGAIN

> ADHD brains don't come with an off switch.
> UNKNOWN

Allow me to say the one thing most people avoid mentioning: systems break. Routines get steamrolled. Laundry multiplies like gremlins. You wake up one morning, and somehow your kitchen looks like it lost a bar fight with a tornado. And your systems? Nowhere to be found. Your brain has simply rejected them completely. Well, that's quite normal. That's the part that no one talks about enough: the backslide. The relapse. The glorious unraveling of all your functional progress.

But here's the thing:

This doesn't mean you failed. It means you're a human being with an ADHD brain, living in a world that doesn't always play fair.

Life throws curveballs like illness, stress, burnout, and surprise field trips, and even the best systems will wobble under the weight of real life. Instead of pretending it will never happen again (been there, lied to myself about that), this chapter is about preparing for the fall and building a soft place to land.

We'll start by normalizing the cycle, and then we'll walk through a simple ritual I call the Sunday scan. This chapter is your reminder that maintenance doesn't have to be military-grade discipline. It can be gentle. Flexible. Forgiving. You are allowed to make a mess and then pick up right where you left off. You're not starting from scratch. No dramatic declarations. Just a little scan, a little tweak, and forward we go. Let's dive in and remember, you're not behind. You're just in a very normal loop.

NORMALIZE THE CYCLE

I want you to repeat the following after me: Backslides are not failures. Come on. Try it! Say it out loud and say it like you mean it.

> *Backslides are not failures!*

Wow, who knew it would be so empowering to be your own cheerleader instead of your worst critic? The truth is, backslides are part of the rhythm of living with ADHD. To view backsliding as failure while living with ADHD is a cruel trick because it sets you up to feel negatively about yourself. But if backslides aren't failures, what are they? They are signs that your system isn't working. It's not a sign of being broken or having failed yet again, but rather a reminder to try something new with your system. They're a sign that you're 100% a human being with a real life and a real nervous system, not just a cleaning robot with unlimited battery life (can you imagine, though?).

Look, I've been down the spiral many times. I've had those days where the laundry is clean but sits in a heap so long that it starts to qualify as a floor cushion. In fact, I once went three full weeks without folding a single towel.

THREE! I pulled clean socks out of the basket like a raccoon every morning, muttering, "I really should get it together." Did that erase the organizational progress I'd made in my home? Nope. Did it mean I had to toss out all my systems and start all over again? Also nope. It simply confirmed what I already knew: When it comes to ADHD, progress is not linear. More often than not, the neurodivergent pattern usually looks something like this:

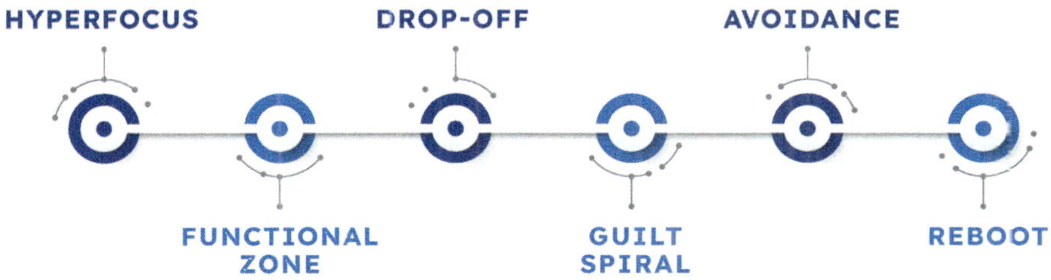

You know what's the best part of this non-linear spiral? It's okay. The key is not letting the drop-off trigger a shame tsunami. According to research on ADHD and emotional regulation, we're more prone to emotional dysregulation, which means those dips can feel much heavier than they are (Shaw et al., 2014). To put it in daily task terms: A neurodivergent and a neurotypical person both get home after a long week. The dishes aren't cleaned, which sparks a pang of frustration. The neurotypical person acknowledges that they would prefer the house to be clean and they feel some emotion toward the situation, but they quickly bounce back as they realize it's not that big of a deal.

The neurodivergent person, on the other hand, feels like a failure. They believe all their progress is out the window and the dishes represent that their life is falling apart. The clutter isn't worse than that of the neurotypical individuals, but the shame is, making it feel impossible to manage. So, what can we do about it? How can we avoid the shame? We can start by reframing dips as emotional checkpoints, and not failure flags. In other words, we can be kind to ourselves and ask, "What does my brain need right now?" instead of "Why can't I just keep it together?"

The reason this simple reframe is so essential is because of what it triggers. When we lean toward the "Why can't I just keep it together" side of things, we are more likely to implement a punishment routine. It sounds extreme, but we're all guilty of it. It's when we add certain activities to our lives to punish ourselves for not keeping it together. For example, the classic "I'll stay up until 2 a.m. to clean everything because I've been slacking this week." The problem with a punishment routine is that it adds to the shame and harshness of the situation. It's not the same as a reset (since a reset is actually helpful). So, instead of entertaining a punishment routine, try one of these recovery rituals instead:

- Light a nice-smelling candle to calm your nervous system.
- Put on a relaxing playlist.
- Clean one square foot of space.
- Sit with your planner for three minutes and notice how you feel and where the tension lies.

These gentle cues tell your nervous system, "We're safe. We can start again." Not from the beginning, just from here. You're not lazy, and you're not destined to live under a mountain of laundry forever. You're managing an executive-function rollercoaster, and sometimes you drop the map for a short bit. It's okay. We have ways to get back on track without self-blame. So, what do you say? Are you ready to normalize the wobbles? Remember, setbacks are part of life, whether you have ADHD or not. With ADHD, they might feel more extreme, but we can choose whether we want to allow the spiral to continue or whether we'll do activities that will help our minds calm down. One of my favorite tools for managing setbacks is what I call the Sunday scan.

THE SUNDAY SCAN

Okay, picture this: It's Sunday. You're sipping coffee (or staring longingly at it while reheating it for the third time). The week's chaos is still clinging to the corners of your space—mail has staged a quiet rebellion on the kitchen counter, and your desk looks like a toddler organized it blindfolded. That's where the Sunday scan comes in handy. What is it? A fast, low-pressure weekly ritual that keeps clutter from becoming a full-blown clutter landslide. It's part mindfulness, part maintenance, and totally doable even in pajamas. We're talking 10 minutes, tops! No cleaning spree. No color-coded spreadsheets. Just a quick check-in with your space to keep things flowing.

The Sunday scan works because it acknowledges that ADHD folks struggle with time blindness and clutter amnesia. It's not about cleaning all surfaces and taking stock of where everything is. Instead, it's about awareness and keeping your executive function from going totally offline. Here's how you can embrace the Sunday scan:

- **Walk through your main living areas:** You don't have to pace like a detective. Just casually stroll through your kitchen, living room, bedroom, and wherever chaos tends to gather. Don't do anything yet and resist the urge to jump into a cleaning frenzy. Be calm, take deep breaths, and just walk through the house.
- **Visually scan or physically touch key surfaces:** Now that you've walked through the house, do it again. This time, touch or visually scan each room more intently. Become aware of which areas are causing you panic and discomfort, and which areas are not so bad. Chances are, "the whole house" isn't such a big mess as you thought. Only one or two areas are really out of hand. Acknowledge which of those areas are currently causing you a headache. Again, resist the urge to start cleaning everything you see.
- **Pick one thing (just one):** Now, choose one, just one, area to clean. Whether it's your kitchen, bedside table, or home office, it's totally up to you. However, stick to one area. The goal isn't to clean the whole house but to simply refresh the worst area. Toss the trash, rehome a few items, and wipe the surface. That's it. No intense vacuuming or deep cleaning the grout. Just a simple, quick refresh.

If your brain is feeling spicy and wants to keep going, that's great. Lean into it, but repeat the process and focus on one other area. Continue like this by committing to one space at a time to prevent feeling overwhelmed. If you're brain isn't feeling spicy, then you're done after one. You've completed the Sunday scan and you're ready for a new week.

The goal of the Sunday scan is to promote consistency. Instead of a deep clean or punishment, we focus on a rhythm of checking in with yourself and your space. If done regularly, the Sunday scan can help you notice things before they get overwhelming. It's almost like brushing your mental teeth. And here's the real magic: Even if your space isn't spotless, doing this consistently builds resilience. It reinforces the story that you are a person who is tending to your space. Even in small ways and even when you don't feel like it, you are taking care of yourself and your space.

However, if you're feeling fried after the week and you're too tired for a Sunday scan, that's okay. Make it smaller. Instead of scanning the whole house in sections, scan only one section. Walk through the living room and identify one thing you can do that will take less than five minutes. Do just that one thing and remember that this is your system. You make the rules, so there's no shame in "breaking" the rules when it's needed. You can also turn the Sunday scan into a game if you need a little extra dopamine. Ask yourself: *Can I find five things to move to the right place in 60 seconds?* Set a timer, play a song, and reward yourself with something fun afterward.

Remember, my fellow ADHDer, your environment is talking to your brain all the time. This Sunday scan can help make sure it's just a soft whisper of encouragement, and not a shouting match.

YOUR SUNDAY SCAN TRACKER

If you want to keep the momentum going, use this mini log to check in with your space once a week. It's not about doing it all, but about showing up, even for five minutes. Check off what you do, skip what you don't, and customize as needed. This is *your* rhythm, so use it as you please.

Weekly Checklist

- ☐ Touched base with the kitchen
- ☐ Cleared one item off the desk
- ☐ Checked the entry/drop zone
- ☐ Picked one surface to scan or wipe
- ☐ Rehomed five things (or even just one!)
- ☐ Did one thing to move the space forward
- ☐ Took a deep breath and reminded myself: "Progress counts, not perfection."

Tip: Stick this list on the fridge, pin it by your front door, or screenshot it for your phone lock screen. That way, it gently raves at you once a week and says, "Hey, we're doing this. Just a little. That's enough." You can also make it yours by adding or swapping tasks that matter to you. Perhaps you want to add wiping the couch or cleaning the remotes. Add whatever task makes you feel like you're taking good care of your space. Additionally, maybe your Sunday scan happens on a Wednesday, and that's totally okay if it works for you. Customize it as much as you need to.

CHAPTER TAKEAWAYS

01 When you experience a backslide, you're not failing. ADHD runs in cycles, and so does home care. Expect the ebb and know the flow will return. Setbacks are not signs that you're broken, but a sign that you're human.

---

02 Shame doesn't spark change, but compassion does. Beating yourself up won't fold the laundry. But talking to yourself kindly might help you toss it in a basket, and that's still progress. Recovery rituals work better than punishment routines, so reach for comfort, not consequence.

---

03 Small scans are more effective than massive overhauls. The Sunday scan is your weekly pulse check for your home, and it doesn't need to be dramatic. Just touch base with your space, do one thing, and walk away with a win.

---

04 Checklists are your nonjudgmental roommate. In other words, use it as a visual accountability buddy and don't see it as a "nag." The checklist doesn't complain or sigh dramatically when you haven't completed it. It just hangs out quietly and says, "You've got this!"

---

05 Progress lives in patterns, not in perfection. One clean counter, one rehomed sock, and one reset ritual can do more than a "perfect" schedule. The small rituals stitch together to make a home rhythm that feels lighter, even when it all falls apart again.

EXCLUSIVE OFFER

I would like you to know that I am committed to helping you thrive with ADHD. Because of that, I am offering you this exclusive offer, which is optional and only complimentary to the contents of this book, in case you want to walk the extra mile.

This is what you will have access to:

1) Ebook: 10 ADHD Decluttering Wins That Take 10 Minutes or Less: This is a collection of cases where ADHD decluttering, cleaning and organizing strategies were implemented successfully, so it could both inspire and motivate you.

2) Print-ready label template: I will be discussing several strategies throughout this book, and some of them involve labeling things around your house. This is to make your journey a little easier. You can download and print it at home or at your preferred store. It is a so pretty easy to customize if you prefer to make any changes and create your own labels.

Scan the QR code below to get access to all of them.

https://amy-harper.kit.com/76f19ed469

THE ADHD SUPPORT MATERIAL YOU NEED..... FOR FREE

EBOOK - 10 ADHD DECLUTTERING WINS THAT TAKE 10 MINUTES OR LESS

- You will get it in two different formats: ebook and pdf.
- That's a quick reference guide for what you can apply today and start seeing some immediate results.
- Real-life stories with tips that can make the difference in your home.

PRINT-READY LABELS FOR YOUR HOME

- Labels are so important, during this book you will learn how to use them.
- I made this template print-ready to make your life as easy as possible.
- Take it, print it at your preferred store or at home, use it.

CONCLUSION

Guess what? You did it! No really. Let it sink in. You did it! Take a moment to sit in this moment and pat yourself on the back for making it to the final chapter of this book. It's no small feat, and you should be proud of yourself. Whether you read straight through like a productivity monster on espresso, or dipped in and out while eating snacks in bed (a personal favorite), the fact remains: You stuck with it!

Why is that such a big deal? Because sticking with anything, especially in the ADHD universe where interest-based nervous systems rule the roost, is basically the equivalent of finishing a marathon while juggling flaming batons. So, give yourself credit. But let's also talk about where you are now.

THE NEW REALITY

Over the course of this book, you've built more than just tidy drawers and dopamine-friendly cleaning rituals. You've started to shape a reality that works for you. A life where your space supports you instead of silently scolding you. A rhythm that follows your energy, your brain, and your life, not a Pinterest fantasy or your third-grade teacher's gold star chart. You now know what functionality looks like in your world. Not perfection. No color-coded bins on every shelf. But a home that gives you a sense of agency. A space that makes it easier to think clearly, breathe deeper, and show up for what matters to you. In other words, you've tapped into pride. Not the kind that makes you want to impress others, but the quiet, gut-level satisfaction types that come from creating systems that don't just look good, but feel good. And that is success!

LET'S REWIND FOR A MINUTE

You started this book curious, or perhaps even frustrated. You wanted to get your home under control, but you were tired of advice that felt like it was written for robots with industrial-strength willpower and a sink with zero dishes. But all of that has now changed (hopefully). I hope you know, with complete confidence, that you were never the problem. The issue was with the systems and not with your brain. To fully embrace the journey you've been on, let's take a moment to look back on and take note of everything we've accomplished over the past twelve chapters. Enjoy the victory lap and take a moment to feel proud of what you've accomplished.

- In Chapter 1, we blew up the myth of laziness and explored the reality of ADHD brains. We looked at how they crave stimulation and resist anything that smells like boredom and shame.
- Next, we explored why clutter comes so naturally to ADHDers. We looked at emotionally charged clutter and how to organize items without building shrines.
- After that, we ditched perfection and embraced a new approach based on "clean enough" standards. Instead of chasing the perfect home, we adopted the idea of accepting a home that is realistic and lived in.
- In Chapter 4, we learned how to stack cleaning in stages, boost our dopamine, and make progress even when energy is low. It was all about cleaning in dopamine-friendly layers, which is a method I fully believe in (and use in my own home).

- Chapter 5 tackled the kitchen and how we can organize a kitchen without trying to turn it into a lifestyle magazine cover shoot. While it might not be aesthetically perfect, it works and it's functional, which is the most important thing. This is where we learned about drop zones and high-use zones for the first time.
- Next, we looked at closets, clothes, and how decision fatigue can contribute to mess. We embraced the idea of building a uniform and how to use a pile system that works.
- After that, it was time to look at the living room and work areas. We explored how to find the balance between reducing visual static without feeling the need to hide everything (because then you'll never find it again).
- In Chapter 8, we chatted about what it's like to share spaces with others. We're all different, and sharing a space can be challenging, but with the right tools and systems, it can also be functional.
- Next, you mastered the art of sneaky habits and attaching a new routine to old ones, making it visual, using dopamine as a motivator.
- After that, you stopped time-blocking your soul into submission and started mapping tasks to your actual energy, having space for low, medium, and high energy levels throughout your day.
- In Chapter 11, we tackled seven bite-sized days of transformation. You cleaned surfaces, created drop zones, conquered drawers, and built rituals that will stick.
- Finally, we looked at what to do when it all falls apart. It's normal to have setbacks, and they don't equate to failure. You learned that setbacks are part of the cycle, which you can learn to ride with grace and recovery tools.

Look at all that. You didn't just declutter. You built momentum and rewired your relationship with your space. You got honest, and you got things done. Well done!

A FINAL SUCCESS STORY FOR THE ROAD

Before we say goodbye, I would like to tell you about Rina.

Rina is a 36-year-old single mom with ADHD who once described her house as a "laundry vortex with snack wrappers." She came to me feeling defeated. "Every time I try to organize, I get super motivated, overhaul everything in one weekend, and then two weeks later it's worse than it was before." Sound familiar?

So, we started small. Rina did a visual reset in her entryway, focusing on just one surface. She texted me a photo and said, "This actually makes me feel like a real adult." From there, she followed the functional freedom sprint, focusing on one day at a time. On the rough days, she used the low-energy options, and it still made a difference. She made her Sunday scan and adopted a bare minimum checklist into her weekly routine. Six months later, she's still using her zones and using energy-mapping. She even told me that it no longer feels like her home is shouting at her. That's what I like to call success. It's not about spotless counters or perfection. It's about peace.

NOW IT'S YOUR TURN

Here's the thing about systems: They evolve. Life changes, routines shift, and new chaos shows up in the form of vacations, illness, and ADHD fog. So, revisit your routines. Re-customize your systems. The frameworks in this book are yours now. Take them, twist them, scale them back, or ramp them up. Do what works for you. This isn't a manual for being a "good" home maker. It's a field guide for building your version of functional freedom, again and again. If one drawer becomes cluttered again, it doesn't mean you failed. It simply means that you've lived. Now, without shame, you can reset and rebuild that drawer until it works the way you want it to.

Let me leave you with this: You're not behind. You're not broken. You're not too messy, too inconsistent, or too much. You are in process and progress. If all you do is rinse a single dish or toss a candy wrapper in the trash, you're still showing up. So go ahead. You've got the tools now! And even if it falls apart, you've got the reset, too.

I'm proud of you! Now go and celebrate your weird, wonderful, ADHD-powered progress. You've earned it.

ACKNOWLEDGEMENTS

This book wouldn't exist without the unwavering support and patience of my better half. Through countless late nights, endless revisions, and moments of self-doubt, you stood by me—offering encouragement when I needed it most. Your belief in my work kept me going, your feedback sharpened my vision, and your quiet strength carried me through. Thank you for being my critic, my cheerleader, my sounding board, and my steady foundation throughout this journey.

REFERENCES

ADDitude Editors. (n.d.). *ADHD and shame: What you need to know.* ADDitude. https://www.additudemag.com/slideshows/adhd-and-shame/

ADDitude Editors. (2021). "ADHD and Object Permanence: Why We Lose Things." *ADDitude Magazine.* https://www.additudemag.com

Allen, D. (2015). *Getting Things Done: The Art of Stress-Free Productivity* (Revised Ed.). Penguin Books.

Anonymous. (n.d.). In *128 Memorable ADHD Quotes.* https://lastingquotes.com/quote-collections/adhd-quotes/

Archer, D. (n.d.). In S. Louise (Ed.), *100+ Uplifting ADHD Quotes for Motivation, Success, and Inspiration.* https://samantalouise.com/adhd-quotes-for-motivation

Ascher, M., & Ascher, L. (2024, May 8). *Overcoming decision fatigue in ADHD.* Psychology Today. https://www.psychologytoday.com/za/blog/changing-the-narrative-on-adhd/202405/overcoming-decision-fatigue-in-adhd

Barkley, R. A. (2011). *Executive Functions: What They Are, How They Work, and Why They Evolved.* Guilford Press.

Barkley, R. A. (2010). *Taking charge of adult ADHD.* The Guilford Press.

Barkley, R. A. (n.d.). In S. Louise (Ed.), *100+ Uplifting ADHD Quotes for Motivation, Success, and Inspiration.* https://samantalouise.com/adhd-quotes-for-motivation

Branson, R. (n.d.). In *100 ADHD Quotes From Experts, Authors and Entrepreneurs.* https://www.adhdflowstate.com/best-adhd-quotes/

Brown, D. (2021). *Organizing solutions for people with ADHD: Tips and tools to help you take charge of your life and home* (2nd ed.). Fair Winds Press.

Brown, T. E. (n.d.). In S. Louise (Ed.), *100+ Uplifting ADHD Quotes for Motivation, Success, and Inspiration.* https://samantalouise.com/adhd-quotes-for-motivation

Cherry, K. (2022, August 17). *What is decision fatigue?* Verywell Mind. https://www.verywellmind.com/decision-fatigue-5215463

Cleveland Clinic. (2022, June 5). *Executive dysfunction: What it is, symptoms & treatment.* Cleveland Clinic. https://my.clevelandclinic.org/health/symptoms/23224-executive-dysfunction

Courage Compass Therapy. (n.d.). *When ADHD is trauma.* https://www.couragecompasstherapy.com/whenadhdistrauma

Davis, K.C. (2022). *How to keep house while drowning: A gentle approach to cleaning and organizing.* Cornerstone.

Finn, A. J. (n.d.). In *80 ADHD Quotes About the Neurodivergent Way of Paying Attention.* https://everydaypower.com/adhd-quotes/

Hallowell, E. M., & Ratey, J. J. (2021). *ADHD 2.0: New science and essential strategies for thriving with distraction—from childhood through adulthood.* Ballantine Books.

Hallowell, E. M. (n.d.). In *80 ADHD Quotes About the Neurodivergent Way of Paying Attention.* https://everydaypower.com/adhd-quotes/

Hallowell, E. M. (n.d.). In S. Louise (Ed.), *100+ Uplifting ADHD Quotes for Motivation, Success, and Inspiration.* https://samantalouise.com/adhd-quotes-for-motivation

Kaufman, S. B. (2021). *Wired to create: Unraveling the mysteries of the creative mind.* Perigee Books.

Kofler, M. J., Sarver, D. E., Harmon, S. L., Moltisanti, A., Aduen, P. A., Soto, E. F., & Ferretti, N. (2017). Working memory and organizational skills problems in ADHD. *Journal of Child Psychology and Psychiatry, 59*(1), 57–67. https://doi.org/10.1111/jcpp.12773

Kooij, J. J. S., Bijlenga, D., Salerno, L., Jaeschke, R., Bitter, I., Balázs, J., & Asherson, P. (2019). Updated European Consensus Statement on diagnosis and treatment of adult ADHD. *European Psychiatry*, 56, 14-34. https://doi.org/10.1016/j.eurpsy.2018.11.001

Littman, E. (2025, March 25). *Never enough? Why ADHD brains crave stimulation.* ADDitude. https://www.additudemag.com/brain-stimulation-and-adhd-cravings-dependency-and-regulation/?srsltid=AfmBOoqHJ7uS7fHKYm6JEhp4zxx0uz2xdAacO67fu5P2Pr8GNbRTgNb6

Neeleman, D. (n.d.). In *100 ADHD Quotes From Experts, Authors and Entrepreneurs.* https://www.adhdflowstate.com/best-adhd-quotes/

Matlen, T. F. (2017). *The queen of distraction: How women with ADHD can conquer chaos, find focus, and get more done.* New Harbinger Publications.

Ovcharenko, J. (2025, January 6). *ADHD & time blindness: What (is it), why (it happens), and how (to fix it?).* Numo ADHD. https://numo.so/journal/adhd-time-blindness

Parker, D. R., & Boutelle, K. (2009). Executive function coaching for college students with learning disabilities and ADHD: A new approach for fostering self-determination. *Learning Disabilities Research & Practice*, 24(4), 204–215. https://doi.org/10.1111/j.1540-5826.2009.00294.x

Psych Central. (2022). *How to clean your home with ADHD: 9 strategies that work.* https://psychcentral.com/adhd/how-to-clean-your-home-with-adhd

Pugle, M. (2024, September 18). *Managing executive dysfunction in ADHD.* Verywell Health. https://doi.org/10.3389/fpsyt.2023.1336040

Russell, B. (2019, October 3). *What is executive function? 7 deficits tied to ADHD.* ADDitude. https://www.additudemag.com/7-executive-function-deficits-linked-to-adhd/

Sharp, M. R. (2024, October 30). *How fidgeting can help people with ADHD focus.* Medical Xpress. https://medicalxpress.com/news/2024-10-fidgeting-people-adhd-focus.html

Shaw, P., Stringaris, A., Nigg, J., & Leibenluft, E. (2014). Emotion dysregulation in attention deficit hyperactivity disorder. *American Journal of Psychiatry, 171*(3), 276–293. https://doi.org/10.1176/appi.ajp.2013.13070966

Silva, S. (2024, October 10). *What is the role of dopamine in ADHD?* Healthline. https://www.healthline.com/health/adhd/adhd-dopamine

Stavraki, I. (2024, February 3). *What is ADHD executive dysfunction?* Simply Psychology. https://www.simplypsychology.org/adhd-executive-dysfunction.html

Unknown. (n.d.). In *110 ADHD Quotes.* https://www.peacefulpolymath.com/2023/03/adhd-quotes.html

Unknown. (n.d.). In *128 Memorable ADHD Quotes.* https://lastingquotes.com/quote-collections/adhd-quotes/

A PLOT TWIST YOU CAN ACTUALLY CONTROL

Hi!

Before you close this book, here's the twist: there's one last step, and it's not mine to take. It's yours.

Most people read a book, close it, and move on. But I have a feeling that's not you. If you're still here, I'd love to ask you for something small but meaningful:

> Would you take a brief moment to share your experience with this book?

Your honest review becomes part of someone else's decision. Someone with ADHD, just like you, is out there scrolling, wondering if this book might help them. Your words could be the nudge that gets them started... or helps them move on. Either way, you make a difference.

Your review may be short, long, anonymous, critical, glowing, messy, thoughtful, whatever feels true.

Just scan the QR code. It'll take you straight to the review page and shouldn't take more than a minute.

Thank you for sticking with me, and for sharing your voice. That's the real ending.

Scan the QR code below.

ALSO BY AMY HARPER

OVERCOMING ADULT ADHD CHALLENGES SERIES

OVERCOMING ADULT ADHD CHALLENGES SERIES

Visit Amazon's Overcoming Adult ADHD Challenges Page and shop for all books. Check out pictures, author information, and reviews for the series.

Printed in Dunstable, United Kingdom

76868649R00107